Sand in my Shoes

Marion Campau McNeil

Todd & Honeywell inc.
Great Neck, New York / 1980

Copyright © 1980 by Marion Campau McNeil
First Edition

All rights reserved. No part of this book may be reproduced in any form whatsoever, except brief passages by a reviewer, without written permission from the publisher.

Published by Todd & Honeywell, Inc.
             Ten Cuttermill Road
             Great Neck, New York 11021

ISBN 0-89962-004-3

Manufactured in the United States of America

Contents

1	Cowlitz Trails	1
2	Comrades All	10
3	For Nights With Stars	16
4	Monte Cristo Trail	18
5	Metaline	24
6	Junior Jack Tars	28
7	Boy's Limbo	34
8	Continental Skyways	43
9	Oregon Trails	53
10	Ne-Ah-Kah-Nie	57
11	Nehalem Nostalgia	62
12	Portland, My Tillicum	63
13	Unknown Village	66
14	Maria and Mabel	71
15	Clouds Flying	73
16	Westport Coast Guard	80
17	A Beacon Seaward	83
18	Peninsula Pete	87
19	The Peninsula, "Lands End"	91
20	My Mail	93
21	Metaline Return	96
22	Alaska	99
23	The Canal and Europe	106
24	Rendezvous In Scotland	110
25	Kaleidoscopic Memories	113
	Aboard the Winnepeg	113
	An Artist's Letters	114
	On Leaving Europe	115
26	Epilogue	116

Acknowledgements

Mr. William G. Kincaide, Chief Boatswain's Mate, U.S.C.G.
Mrs. H. M. Delanty
Florence K. Lewis, Aberdeen Library, Aberdeen, Wn.
Pilot David Russell Bath, West Coast Air Lines
Mr. and Mrs. Richard Karnowski, Westport, Washington
Washington Historical Society
College of St. Scholastica, Duluth, Minnesota
Irvine T. Seath, *Aberdeen World*
William P. Koski, *Grays Harbor Washingtonian*
Mr. and Mrs. Joe Lindstrom, Westport, Washington
Mrs. Grace Gardner, Seattle, Washington
Lt. (j.g.) Harry E. Helegeson, Astoria, Oregon
Mr. John Waddingham, *Oregon Journal*
Detroit Public Library, Detroit, Michigan
Mr. Charles J. Pierce, 11 Bond Way, London, England SW8 ISJ

Bibliography

A Brief Sketch of Grays Harbor — Edward Van Sickle
Along the Waterfront — Ret. Lieut. Com. H. M. Delanty
Beeswax and Gold — Thomas H. Rogers
Washington, The Evergreen State — Binsford & Mort
Legends and Traditions of N.W. History, "Legend of Lost Galleons" — Hon. Glenn M. Ranck
The Story of Nehalem — by Cotton

Dedication

TO THE MEMORY OF MY FATHER
Edward Sylvester Campau
Who bequeathed to me his joy of life.

"Feet to follow with and wings to bring me home."

1
Cowlitz Trails

From my cabin window
Richly tinted patterns
Traced against the blue
Dark or gold-flecked emerald
And a silver hue.
Where the shadows linger
Now as twilight comes,
They will change to greyness
When the night wind thrums
At my cabin window.
I shall watch them limned
On the sky in blackness,
All their glory dimmed
By the swift dark magic,
But perhaps I'll see
Midnight pouring amber gold
Through a mountain tree!

The summer following my graduation was spent largely in seeking my first teaching post. I was indeed a novice and at that time it was exceedingly hard to get one's very first school—the year is 1923.

Father gave up a lot of good fishing week-ends to the boring task of driving me around to make personal applications whenever possible. I didn't find anything I liked near home and I had never been away from home.

I dreamed of going to some far distant place where I would have all kinds of adventures. I sat for hours with the map of Washington spread out on my lap, picking the farthest and most remote places to write applications to.

The mail was something to look forward to after the wearisome hours of letter writing. Many wrote back, "Sorry to inform you but we have succeeded in employing an EXPERIENCED teacher." But finally the glowing morning when with trembling fingers I opened just one more reply. The tears rolled slowly down my cheeks, when Oh, joyous day! I had been accepted!

I danced a merry jig as I looked all over the house for mother, who I found out in the back yard hanging up the wash. Mother said, "Now don't get too excited, you might really not like it there."

My very first school was characteristically enough, 'The Little Mountain School,' located in the watershed of the Cowlitz and Kalama rivers, and my post office address was to be Carrolls, Washington.

So I wanted adventure!

I went down there on the train from Seattle. It was just a whistle stop. I was to be met at train time, but there was no one to meet me.

I went in to the general store there to make inquiry. The proprietors told me in exceedingly bored voices that they didn't know anything about anybody meeting anyone. I walked around and around out in front of the store, trying to make up my mind what to do. Finally I was told that if I waited long enough maybe someone might show up. I waited all afternoon!

At near closing time a young boy appeared very little younger than myself. He drove me what seemed miles and miles up into the hills from the railroad station. We stopped with a family he knew for the night because when we reached there it was pitch dark and too late to go any farther that day.

I could see that the house was none too clean and I hardly slept at all because I was worried about the bedding.

We arose early the following morning. The young boy, whom I knew now as Joe, got two horses for us. That is, one was his horse that he had left there the day before, and the other horse was for me. My suitcase was strapped on the one I was to ride. After assisting me to mount, Joe got on the other horse. (I was glad now for my single previous experience on a horse.)

I was quite delighted, and thought to myself how much more thrilling this was than the hum-drum life at home. We rode thus for miles and miles. After several hours of this, I asked Joe every so often if we weren't nearly there. He finally assured me that we should reach there before dark!

Our route over a virgin trail in the forest became steeper and steeper. Then storm clouds appeared out of nowhere, it began to thunder and lightning and the rain came down in sheets. My left leg began to feel quite numb as part of the weight of the suitcase was on it, and I was wet now to the skin.

Joe got off his horse from time to time to readjust the straps so I wouldn't be so uncomfortable. My thought was: so I wanted adventure! I was near to tears but reflected they probably wouldn't want a crying 'school marm.'

At about dusk when I thought I couldn't stand one minute more of this unglamorous ride, Joe said, "We'll be there in about half an hour."

The deluge of rain had somewhat let up by this time but I was so numb by then that nothing seemed to matter.

Then wonder of wonders—we came out into a clearing and I could see a large barn and a small log cabin, with a lean-to on the back of it. We rode the horses right up to the porch of the cabin. I took heart then even though I looked and was just like a wet floor mop.

Joe's mother, a kindly woman, appeared and made haste to make me as comfortable as she could. I was given a very delicious dinner of fried rabbit. During the meal, however, I felt like a gold fish and a guinea pig all rolled into one. I was being watched covertly by the woman's husband. I was exhibit A, B, C and D.

During the conversation of the evening, I inquired where the school was and was told that it was only a mile and a half away and that Joe would take me over there in the morning.

Came morning and a huge breakfast, much more than I was in the habit of eating, I was taken over to the school. Little was I prepared for the very strenuous walk involved. We were walking a virgin trail. Some trees had fallen since the trail had been cleaned out. Steps had been cut over some of the largest trees. One that we climbed over was at least six feet or more in diameter.

I recall one place where we had to roll over on our bellies as no steps had been cut in that one. My legs at one point proved a little unsteady negotiating the other side, while looking dizzily down for a new footing.

At last we came out to a clearing where I saw an old log cabin with the roof caved in. Joe explained that this was the 'old school house.'

With some misgivings I wondered what the 'other' would be like.

I was not too disappointed when the little 'new' school house came into view. It was a portable building consisting of one classroom with a cloakroom at the back. It was painted white. There was a flag pole, and the flag had been hoisted and was blowing stiffly in the breeze. It seemed to have an air of expectancy, and I was very happy about it.

I had five pupils that winter. Grades two, five, seven and the first year of high school. This high school business was a complete surprise and I had to study every night to keep one lesson ahead of my pupil, in Algebra, English and Ancient History.

My castle that winter was the lean-to on the back of the log cabin. It was a small room built of hand split cedar shakes. It contained a single cot, an air-tight stove, a wash stand, two chairs and a bearskin rug. I ate with the family and used the common living room. The mountain life was a real innovation and initiation for me. All that I had known about nature in the raw I had found between the covers of a book.

One day when Joe and I came home from school, his mother said, "We'll have to go after the cow; she hasn't come home yet and I am afraid she has had her calf today."

All this seemed far removed from my experience and so I asked if I might go along. We covered considerable distance over the usual range, then we went down into a ravine. It had started to rain and the wind was blowing coldly when we suddenly came upon her.

The calf was standing up weakly and it was still wet. The cow was licking it, and a part of the afterbirth was still hanging from the mother. It was strung along over the brush for some distance.

Joe picked up the calf and strode slowly up the side of the ravine. His mother followed behind, gently urging the cow along. The sight of the afterbirth was slightly nauseating to me as I had no idea about anything like that.

We got them both home and in the barn. They let the calf suck from the mother until the third day, then they separated them and fed the calf from a can. I heard it bawling the first few nights and I could hardly go to sleep for thinking of the poor little calf!

Every evening I went to the barn with Joe while he milked. The whole experience was part of a new life for me. The only thing that I was really afraid of was their turkey gobbler who met me menacingly at the gate each night.

The school itself was rather boring with such a few pupils, after I had had so many in the training school.

One of the boy pupils was sub-normal and it was annoying to have to waste time on him that could have been better employed in working with the other students, my high school pupil, for instance.

One very difficult day I told him to go home (not knowing, in the center of this forest, what else to do with him). He could not have been punished in a normal way, as due to his condition, no point would be gained.

I didn't give the matter any thought the rest of the afternoon. At the close of school I went down the trail with the others a short distance, as I had been in the habit of doing. What was my chagrin to see his staring eyes looking out at me from behind a stump. I said to him, "Why didn't you go home?"

He was speechless, then I was indeed sorry for him, because I then realized, on further reflection, that he didn't have enough sense to find his way home alone. This was surely a spot where I had shown my inexperience.

One week-end I was begged by the children to come to stay with them for the week-end. All my pupils were members of the same family except Joe. I wasn't overly anxious to go but decided I had better go to save their feelings. It turned out that I stayed only the first night. In my preparations to go I said to Joe, "Now you bring my horse, which you will pretend was lost and that you went hunting for; and call for me, the chances are they'll not take a tumble."

It was a good thing that I had made this arrangement as the filth that I ran into was indescribable. They lived as the poorer white trash of the Virginia mountains are known to live. Even the dishes were so dirty that eating was nauseating. And the bed which I shared with the older girl! The odor of it was enough!

In the middle of the night I pretended that I rolled out of bed. I got down on the floor and put my coat over me!

There were other much pleasanter experiences.

When the snow was on, we went tobogganing down the side of the mountain, while staying week-ends at the home of some friends of Joe's.

Then there were the mountain hoe-downs. Getting ready for one of these, I said to Joe, "What if it rains after the dance when we are on the way home?"

He answered, "Well, you won't have to worry about that because we won't be coming home until the next day."

This was a shock, but I didn't say anything. I just wondered what my parents would have thought.

Going, we rode horseback down the mountain then, joining another family, we rode the rest of the way in the back of a truck filled with hay.

We rode for miles and at last came to a rather dingy looking mountain cabin that looked like an Indian 'longhouse.'

As we entered, I noticed that there was very little light, just kerosene lamps in brackets around the room. There was an old man fiddler and an accordion player.

As the party progressed I noted that every once in a while they got up and went outside. I was so green that I didn't realize that they were bolstering their playing with the 'hoochiest of hooch.'

I did take one drink out of politeness. I knew they were trying out the new teacher. They drank neat and I had never had anything like it in my life before.

About three A.M. a delicious supper was served. At first I thought, how boring! I'll never be able to stay awake all night.

I found, however, that I learned to do a 'hoe-down' with the best of them. At times I laughed so hard that I thought I would never be able to stop.

Riding up the mountain again in the cool dawn, sleep almost overcame me, as it was the first time in my life that I had ever stayed up ALL night!

Another time I rode over to stay the week-end with the wife of the clerk of the school board, the husband being away. This woman hadn't seen anyone for months. She was so glad of company, especially someone new, that she talked all through the first night. We went to bed at noon the next day, when there was a sudden downpour of rain. It was pleasant to sleep in the attic hearing the rain on the roof, the wind blowing so heavily outside.

My hostess had a lot of cute kittens and I felt like putting a few in my pocket to take home.

The 'piece de resistance' that week-end was bear steak which she had canned herself. She was the very best kind of a cook and made an oldfashioned bear pot-pie that was very good.

Before he had a chance to hear what I was going to say, I lifted my arms, dumping the whole pail of water over him!

His mother who was standing there in the kitchen, exclaimed, "Sacred Mother of Mary! Preserve us!"

She really was a good sport and liked me alot, as likewise did Joe, or I never would have gotten away with it.

Spring plowing gave me another mode of self-expression. It would, to the casual observed, have seemed a bit undignified, but I followed the plow with my bare feet, just to get the feel of the freshly turned earth. This experience was in a class by itself.

One day in the late spring I decided I would stay over later at the school house and make a new border for the blackboard. I hit the trail for home just as it was beginning to get dark. Darkness seemed to drop down out of nowhere. I made the wrong turn in the trail.

The familiar markings were not so easily discernible in the fading light.

I walked and walked for miles it seemed to me. Suddenly I heard a soft padding on the trail ahead of me. In the faint glimmer of disappearing light, I could just make out a cub bear.

I followed him very slowly for some distance, being careful to make as little noise as possible. This was the first bear I had ever seen out of captivity. To say that I was frightened would be an understatement. Just then my little wild baby jumped off the trail into the brush.

I began to realize that I must retrace my steps until I came back to the place where I had made the wrong turn. This I did and to my great joy I found the regular branching of the trail. On and on I went. It was so very dark that I reasoned the only way I could keep the trail was to watch for the skyline over the treetops. Following this sky trail, I reached my safe haven at last. I was happy to know that I had kept my wits about me, and had not gotten too panicky.

Several weeks later there came a knock on the school door. It was a representative of a newsreel company. The man asked me if I would have any objection to riding with Joe over some of this scenic area. He wanted to get some shots that wouldn't then be called 'dead scenery.'

We both agreed to this readily. The trip was arranged for the following day, which happened to be Saturday. I didn't feel too glamorous so if he took anything close up, I would give them my best smile. This I would probably do anyway, as I would be 'doing what comes naturally.'

He took some interesting shots which are the usual scenes they capture in a travelogue. He had already on his reel, the side flashes to intersperse, of the very cute little chipmunk as it went zipping to the very top of one of the highest trees.

We had some laughs to ourselves after it was over, and at the end of our trip we had pocketed enough money to make up for the time spent.

As I put behind me my adventures over Cowlitz trails, I would always remember the things that I had learned here. These would be remembrances to cherish, until that nebulous day when I might have a cabin of my own choosing, resting picturesquely on some far and as yet unknown mountain trail, where through my cabin window I might see, 'midnight pouring amber gold through a mountain tree.'

Other week-ends I rode out along the mountain trails with one of my new acquaintances, a logger with one glass eye. He was a fine looking man, and I was grieved to learn about his eye. We rode in an area that several years previously had been burned over by forest fires. As we rode along we came to the huge whitened stubs of former forest giants that were still standing.

We took along a pair of field glasses. When we stopped for lunch, tying our horses, we saw long vistas of virgin timber to the distant purpled rim where the sky met the trees. We caught occasional glimpses of deer, bear and other wild animals.

One of these times we rode along the banks of the upper Coweeman River. When we came to a shallow place we went swimming. I was dared to swim across; the current was very strong in places but I could not afford to lose a bet, especially this one! I did get across but had to rest before attempting the return trip.

At this time I wrote long letters home telling my parents how uninspiring I thought civilization was with all its artificialities!

This came as quite a shock to them.

I can recall, too, how on my first visit 'outside,' the city traffic annoyed me. The most wonderful thing in my life then was wanting to get back to 'thum thar hills,' and AWAY from the city!

Father didn't like it at all when he heard me say that I was going to buy a log cabin and live all alone on the side of a mountain. I suppose he thought: all this education, and for what?

Father had to go down to Portland on business and he was taking Mother along. They wrote that if I cared to go, I could get on the train at MY WHISTLE STOP.

I made connections all right. I inquired for Mother and Father, and learned that they were in the parlor car. As I sped rapidly through the cars, the people sitting and lolling about in the seats seemed so indolent to me that my thought was: WHY DON'T THEY GET OUT IN THE WORLD AND DO SOMETHING?

My beloveds were wearing rather aggrieved expressions when I got there. I found out that my manner of dress was very obnoxious to their sense of the fitness of things. They were dressed to the gills, Mother all freshly coiffed, etc., and there was I, pants, wool socks and high laced boots notwithstanding!

They remonstrated with me, but they found a hardened, obdurate, country rustic under the shell of what had once been me.

One morning in the dead of winter there was a heavy fall of snow. Joe went on ahead to break trail to the schoolhouse. It was an almost superhuman task to make way over an already arduous trail. We finally reached our destination in what appeared to be a distant lost and changed world, covered with fairy land sparkles.

There were the minute trackings on the snow of small birds and burrowing animals. All was very silent. No sound broke the stillness!

We came to the front of the schoolhouse and tried the front door. We could not get it open because it was frozen shut.

I thought Joe was only kidding me and just wanted to get out of going to school. I didn't believe him so I said, "Let's go around to the back."

We went around and managed to get in the back door. When Joe started the fire, I began to feel all funny and dizzy coming from the intense cold outside. Being an inexperienced winter traveler, I insisted on sitting much too near the stove.

"I believe I'm going to faint," I said.

I sat down and Joe began unlacing my boots, I was sinking down into an abyss, then everything blacked out!

When I came to Joe was rubbing one of my feet slowly. Then he said, "I was afraid you weren't going to come to, and I was wondering what I was going to do."

The laced boots were the very worst thing I could have had on in this contingency, and their lacings had stopped the circulation. (The next time I wore riding boots with three pairs of woolen socks.)

The other children put in no appearance so it was evident that there would be no school that day.

It stormed for three more days. It was a week before we hit the trail again. This time the other children came and we made a chain gang to force open the frozen shut back door.

During the times at home, Joe and I enjoyed the companionship of each other, and he teased me considerably. One time when he had me just about ready to cry, I decided to fool him. I put a very innocent expression on my face as I went to the well for one of my usual pails of water. I thought I'd pass through the kitchen and call to him, with the pail of water in my hand, I said, "Did you ever hear this one?"

2

Comrades All

I returned to the university in the fall. That winter I put in more work toward my degree.

My next assignment was a small school at Whitney Spit, in the region of Dabob Bay, on Hood's Canal. The leading industry here was the plant of the Bee Lumber Company.

The school was very small and left much to be desired. There were three families there, all related. I boarded around, spending several months with each of the families.

Whitney Spit was reached only by a small boat, there being no boat in there at the time. If one happened to be in the mood and had the time, it was a three mile walk along the shore line which could be traversed only at low tide, on account of overhanging cliffs.

There was an interesting family there, the Lloyds, who were very old-fashioned. The father of the family could play the mouth organ and knew many of the old tunes I had heard my own father play.

Often in the evenings I planned a program for the children. After they had all done their stunts, Mr. Lloyd played for us. We did the Virginia Reel and other square dances.

The pride of the Lloyds was their little steamboat in which they made short runs week-ends, and went down to Quilcene to put in grocery supplies and do other shopping. It was quite a novelty to me as it was woodburning. I had never been on such a craft. We were stalled once out in the middle of Dabob Bay with a heavy sea blowing up. Mr. Lloyd had the patience of Job and we managed to make port in safety.

There was a lodge for summer tourists called Linger Longer Lodge down at the end of the bay. I often hiked down there along the beach at low tide. I was anxious not to miss the dances held there on Saturday nights. The high school teachers who were teaching at Quilcene stayed at the Lodge. It seemed heaven to me to be with other people after the isolation, coupled with the unadulterated companionship of just the three families at Whitney Spit.

Among other attractions at the Lodge was the piano—there was none where I was staying—and music had always played such a prominent part in my life. We all played for each other. One of the favorites was the "Love Ship" which later proved to be a good theme song for me.

There was a particular night that the other teachers said, "There are two boys coming down tonight, and one of them is very anxious to meet you."

Upon being introduced, I found myself looking at someone I thought I must always have known. We danced the first dance together, and the next and the next. It seemed hard to be parted even for the circle two-step. Every time we met in the circle he squeezed my hand until he worked his way around to me again. He was very neat appearing and was the only fellow there wearing a white shirt and black tie. This was the kind of man I had always dreamed about.

The meeting of Paul and me was the beginning. We were together every week-end. When it was too stormy for him to make the crossing in the boat, he hiked along the beach to meet me.

One Sunday morning we had a narrow escape. The tide was moving up on us rapidly. Sometimes we didn't get it timed just right for hiking. We approached the log chute which extended from the camp down into the Sound. Paul said, "We'll have to hurry up, honey, you know the logs might start shooting down here any minute now."

I looked at the width of the chute. It looked pretty slippery to me and it was about six feet or more across. It was so greasy that I thought neither one of us would be able to stand up. Reaching the outer edge, we got down on our knees and rolled over the outer master log on our stomachs.

We had just managed to clear the chute when a log came booming down, hitting the water in a shower of spray. It was foolhardy to have crossed the chute at that time but the tide was coming up on us and we had no alternative.

Upon reaching the lodge, we both took showers and got ourselves cleaned up from the log chute adventure. Later in the evening we attended the dance which was in Irondale that Saturday.

Before we parted that night, it was decided that we would both go to Seattle. We would go together! The school term was not up yet. I would make some excuse about there being illness in the family or something. We were very much in love and the thought of marriage was uppermost in our minds.

I left Whitney Spit the following Friday, taking just one piece of baggage with me. Paul was to meet me at the lodge. I crossed the bay in an open boat and rowed myself to the lodge as Paul would not get off early enough to come that far. The man at the house where I had been staying said, "I don't want you to go; it will be too rough today. I am sure something will happen to you if you go out with that sea running. Please don't go until morning; I don't want to take the responsibility!"

I looked out at the thundering surf. Prevailing upon him, I said, "Oh, I can manage a boat all right. I am not afraid, anyway, God will take care of me."

He finally agreed to launch the boat and I rowed across this angry bit of bay. I was very frightened but I didn't let the man know or he never would have let me go.

Paul was waiting on the beach at the lodge to pull the boat up. He had been watching me bobbing up and down, now visible, now disappearing behind huge waves. When I was safely on shore he was almost overcome to see that I was safe at last.

I had left some things at the lodge over the many weekends I had been coming and going. These we crammed into an extra suitcase. We both sat on the suitcase to get it shut. Then we drove to Quilcene where we got the bus for Seattle. Although Mother and Father had heard all the details of the affair, they were hardly expecting us to put in such a sudden appearance. Knowing me, Father could understand a whole lot better than anyone else.

There followed a month of going out every single night. We simply 'did' the town. Although I had been in Seattle all my life, there were many places I had never been.

Nightclubbing. I had never been! What a novelty! Paul often teased me because I wasn't used to keeping such late hours. He called me his 'Sleepy Time Gal' every time he saw that I was getting sleepy.

By the end of this perfect month, we had spent considerable money. It was necessary for him to get something else to do as we planned to be married in the late summer.

Paul had worked on an oil tanker previous to his work in the woods, so he got a job with the Associated Oil Company, running between California ports, Seattle, and points in Alaska.

Life was indeed an empty thing with Paul on the high seas. I existed, but did not live, except in the moments when his letters would arrive.

We had a little mascot in the person of a small kewpie doll. She was dressed in a large purple picture had, and trailed a long formal gown. She was only about six inches tall and was not one of those cheap carnival dolls. She was purchased at a church bazaar. I called her the "Beale Street Mama." She reminded me of a very wicked lady all dressed up.

Paul took her on the boat with him when he went away. She was for good luck. He kept her in a prominent place in his stateroom. When writing to me he always referred to her, giving her reactions to everything. He referred to her as the B.S.M. One of his letters read:

"Hello, Marion dear, how's the world treating you today? I just got through the disagreeable task of packing a drunk man aboard and putting him to bed (the wireless operator). That's the most excitement we've had since I joined this barge and it helps some to break the endless monotony. Even things we dislike most can serve as diversion at times. You know, such times as, when our minds have kept turning over a single subject until we're nearly crazy.

"The wireless operator diverts his mind by getting scupperly, I mine, by packing him aboard. Isn't it kind of him?

"Do you know I am just as anxious as can be to get back to 'Frisco' and a letter from you. To find out what you're doing and how everything is while I'm away. It's a fact, and if there isn't a letter there for me I won't be responsible for my actions in any way, shape or form. It's the truth, there's only one thing on earth as lonesome and dreary as being at sea away from everything and everyone the heart holds dear, and that's being ashore in the same predicament!

"It certainly is a wonderful night on the river. The stars are all out, everyone of them, and the water is just as still as, well nothing can be stiller than water when it is still, or show the strife of the world more truly and vividly when it is wrought up. But that's another subject.

"What was on my mind was how pleasant a boat ride would be under the right conditions. Do you agree? Impossible! Well, my poor mind has contracted the habit of harboring impossibilities of late, so you see how it is.

"Beale Street Mama: I sure feel sorry for her, forced to stay aboard this old wagon with nothing to associate with but men, it's awful. I know she's lonesome even though I do the best I can by her. One has nothing on the other, as we both do the best we can, that's all a mule can do. "There's much talk aboard this misery trap (always is) about the next trip being to Seattle, but it's nothing to be depended on.

"B.S.M. sends her love with mine,

>Always,
>Paul."

Paul was at sea the better part of three months, and had been in Seattle off and on. He made his final trip to Alaska, writing me every other day. He was due in Seattle in about two weeks.

Four days went by and no letter. Then more days. I began to be frantic. I listened for his step on the porch every night. I listened to the chiming of the clock and wondered how many hours would chime away before he would come or send some word.

One night about midnight, I heard a step on the porch, just as I was preparing to go upstairs to bed. I opened the door, there stood a boy with a telegram in his hand.

It was from the Associated Oil Tanker, W. F. Herrin. It read:

"We regret to inform you that Paul B. ____ met with an accident, and was washed overboard!" Other explanatory details followed.

So it was done! DONE! It just couldn't be. This happened to other people but not to me. I sat down slowly not knowing what I was doing. No tears came, but a wave of the most awesome loneliness I had ever experienced came over me.

I must have sat there for hours with the telegram in my hands. Mother and Father were sleeping soundly upstairs and knew nothing about it.

In a phantasmagoric flash, our whole acquaintance and times we had together came vividly to mind. One scene merged quickly into another, then it seemed that I could feel the terrible surge of wind and water, the mountainous waves, that had swept him overboard.

In my mind I went down into an abyss of darkest night. I was numb! Numb!

Some one was shaking me.

"Marion, Marion, what's the matter?" It was my Father bending over me.

I had sat out the night in the chair, the telegram was still clutched in my hand!

Days followed days. Days with no ending and no beginning.

The family moved to a new home shortly after this. I had no desire to see any of my friends. If anyone came to see me I could not hold back the tears. I would ask to be excused. To me life was ended. Ended!

Often thereafter there came to mind an expression Paul had often quoted to me. It was taken from Owen Meredith's "Lucille":

"We but catch at the skirts of the thing we would be, and fall back in the lap of a false destiny."

I never had realized the thought behind that quotation before. It came to mind so vividly now!

3

For Nights With Stars

One summer I worked in sports, for the Camp Fire Girls at Camp Sealth on Puget Sound.

It was a varied activity; there were riding and swimming groups, also mountain trips and some trips made by water. One of the yachting trips and some trips carried us up through the San Juan Islands. A stop was made at Victoria, B.C., where we swam in the Crystal Gardens and had Tea at the Empress.

Crossing the Straits of Juan de Fuca, the side to side roll, surge and shudder of our craft didn't mix too well with the activity of frying bacon. Some of us danced on the fore-deck of the ship as it spun along. Later in the day, the queasy feeling and the frying of the bacon became a distant memory.

The Council Fires at Camp Sealth were held on the top of a high hill overlooking the main camp. This hill we called "Heaven." Nothing is more inspiring than the memory of the firelight against the fir trees and the night sky, shining on the happy faces of the girls who were gathered here to be awarded their honors.

There was something sublime in the memory of the close of this ceremonial. The winking lights of the many tiny candles carried by each girl as the yearly procession wound slowly down this forested hill to the hall where the final banquet of the season was held.

The winking lights represented in a way the promises for the future for each one of these girls. It was a thing set apart to have had the privilege of this intimate relationship.

Envied nights were possibly the nights when after taps, as a quiet moon rose over the waters, the girls from Shining Sky Camp came to serenade each unit, the voices carried softly by the lapping tide. If I could have transferred myself to a Venetian loggia on the Grand Canal, the effect could not have been more heartwarming, serene and melodious!

4

Monte Cristo Trail

We've found a wilderness,
Where countless peaks
Rear awe-inspiring crowns,
Pearl-tipped with silver mist
And robed in April hues, sunkissed,
Far, far from towns.
—Grace Gardner

During that summer, my parents urged me to go on different trips offered by friends, to help me forget this poignant part of my life.

Katherine Knowlton, known as the "Lady of Monte Cristo," asked me if I was adept at making a mountain pack without a regular pack board. Also, 'could I hike any distance without pulling the tenderfoot act.' I answered that she should try me.

Thus it was decided that I should join her and a friend of hers on a trek to Barlow Pass. She was going to do some of the regular checking on her claims. We planned on staying there at least for the week-end.

The first part of the trip was made by car, going up by way of Marysville and Granite Falls. Early in the same afternoon, we had reached the place called "Suzy's" at Verlot. Here we stopped for lunch, driving on later to the Big Four Inn. This was as far as the road went at that time. After a short stop for friendly conversation, we left the inn.

We left the car at the inn and entered a narrow foot path which was the approach to the main trail. The trail was profusely overgrown with an interlacing of ferns of all kinds. We started the trip filled with general well being and an anticipation of what might await us around any turn.

Miss Knowlton walked ahead of us as she was thoroughly familiar with every landmark and wrinkle on the trail. We started at a pace which she considered slow, but we thought was plenty fast enough. It was very winding and became increasingly difficult as we progressed.

We carried oddly assorted packs. 'Slippy,' which I had dubbed Miss Knowlton's friend, was carrying a sleeping bag in which were all her groceries. My pack was made into a poncho and consisted of three blankets inside of which were rolled three cans of soup, a box of crackers, a loaf of bread and three cans of canned milk and a sweater.

It was rolled the long way of the blankets. Each end was tied, then the two ends were tied together, the loop part rested on my shoulder, with the tying appearing at the hip line. This was meant to balance the weight more evenly. The load could then be reversed from shoulder to shoulder when one side became tired.

To make way was the task of a real trailer as the trail was overhung and partly indistinguishable in some places. We came to much fallen timber and slippery clay based terrain. There were places where we had to throw over our packs, roll over on our bellies, then retrieve the packs afterwards.

As time passed the angle over which we proceeded became increasingly steep. After two or more hours of this progress, we came to intermittent smoother places where it was not necessary to break trail.

In one area we walked the old road-bed of an abandoned railway, sometimes referred to as the "Rockafellow Road." It had been put in in the hey-day of the Monte Cristo mines. The ties were crumbling to decay. Some were already part of the surrounding soil. Others were moss and lichen covered.

We followed these for quite some time, at last coming to an old trestle spanning a river. Across this there now was resting only one narrow plank. We must cross this!

I looked down to the rushing turbulent river hundreds of feet below as it crashed through a narrow gauge in the rocks. I wondered how we were going to cross it.

With easy nonchalance, Miss Knowlton went over. She was accustomed to making this trip at regular intervals, even in the early fall before the great snows came.

Slippy went over next. She was warned not to look down, that it would be much easier for her if she didn't. She stopped in the middle of the span, giggling nervously, saying, "How'm I doing?"

"Don't try to put one foot ahead of the other, just shuffle along, and DON'T LOOK DOWN," came from Miss Knowlton.

At last there was Slippy, all safe and sound!

I thought, if she can do it I can. I was scared to death, and told the others not to watch me, that if they even cracked a smile, and I got to laughing that there would just be a big POW! as I would hit the water.

They tried their very best, turning their faces away until I had got past the middle. NOW I did not dare to put one foot ahead of the other. A tight rope walker could have managed. There was I—too frightened to continue. One of them offered to come out after me, but I thought no, if I lose my balance we'll BOTH go over together.

I told them to go ahead and pretend that I was already across, I would join them in a few minutes. I stood there pensively, alone for these few minutes. I offered up a little prayer, then I gingerly shoved my left foot up behind my right every time my right slid forward, all the time I watched ahead and not DOWN.

At last there I was safely on the other side. I was so overcome with emotion that slow tears were easing themselves down my cheeks.

Now we got out thermos bottles and had coffee while resting. If they noticed anything unusual in my expression they did not refer to it. There was a long quiet pause for all of us. I kept perfectly still as Father would have said, 'for once.' I guess I had earned my right not to be called a TENDERFOOT!

The trail seemed endless as we plunged doggedly onward through a tangle of overhanging vines. Ominous clouds began to gather. We wondered if we would make camp before it began to rain. Now it began to thunder and jagged arrows of lightning broke across the sky. We speeded up our pace all we could.

Then came the rain, a swift, powerful downpour that soon soaked us up to the waist. The brush did the rest by slapping us around the head and shoulders. No one said much now. I suppose Miss Knowlton thought, 'I had better sympathize with these *"couriers du bois"* or we'll never make camp." On and on, no magic cloak to whirl us to our destination! If Grandmother had been along she would have used one of her stock phrases, "My, what weather!"

It wasn't long before we came to an abandoned camp. It had been deserted several years previously for lack of a road to get supplies in. Here we rested. We made a fire in the stove, drying our clothes out some. I thought it would have been wonderful just to stay here for the night. There was a lovely balcony that overhung the river which I thought would have been fun to sleep in.

It was decided, however, that we must go on. Now it was increasingly difficult to walk as we were very tired and far from really dry. Then we got all wet over again as we hit the trail. Ah! those wet ferns shoulder high. As time wore on they seemed like greedy clutching fingers that begrudged our entry into their wilderness. The rain continued to pour down in sheets. No place here for the tenderhearted!

Poor Slippy (she had earned that moniker for wearing, above all things for a mountain trip, rubber boots!). A colored lady I used to know would have said, "De po' chile, she jest slip back ev'y step she take."

It was nobody's dream. We plunged on, we were too tired for further communication and it began to get dark with a faint reverberation of distant thunder to windward. If we could have sung the soldier's song from "The Vagabond King," "Tramp, tramp, tramping down the highway" we would have been better off, but there was no song in us.

Slippy, with now a frowning look up ahead, was getting ready to pull the mule act. With her boots she had taken two steps to every one of ours. But she was naturally a lighthearted soul and had been the life of the party up until the going was bogged down with this downpour. She looked and motioned to me the give-up signal. I shook my head back at her, giving the Yiddish sign of it's-no-go, rolled my eyes skyward and pointed meaningfully UP the trail.

No, we would not give up now that we had almost reached the end of the trail. We put on our flashlights to find footing and trudged on. At last there came a break in the trees overhead and Miss Knowlton said, "We are just about there."

We came out onto a flat clearing. At one side there were two well built cabins and, farther back, there was a lean-to. We followed our leader as she made rapid strides toward it. We were in the last stages of hikers that don't give up. We flashed our lights as we approached. For a minute no one said anything.

We noted a fire burning in a small stove, casting its reflections toward the ceiling of split shakes. We couldn't see much until we got up a little closer.

A man who had been checking claims had been hurt. He was lying on his back fully clothed. We had no idea what had happened to him; we wondered at first why he was so quiet. There was no glad hand extended.

Filled with self pity, we thought we were the ones who had done the work in coming up all that long way!

Investigation proved that he had fallen backward over a log in dense undergrowth. He had wrenched his back so severely that he could hardly move. He was also out of tobacco, which is a trial to a man at a time like that.

We broke out our supplies but we were so tired that we didn't prepare much of a meal. We made coffee however, and a good clam chowder. This we ate with huge quantities of fresh bread.

After we had finished, we went over to the ranger's cabin, where we were introduced to the ranger and his wife. They were very cordial and did all they could to make us feel at home. we talked until the wee hours. Later we were taken to an adjoining cabin for the night.

Our main difficulty was that all of our clothing was drenched and we had no dry ones to change to. The ranger's wife took our clothes over to her cabin to dry them out. She also made our bunks up. She heated some large rocks, putting them at the foot of the beds. The only thing really dry that we had with us were our coat sweaters that had been in our bed rolls. These we buttoned around our hips as we got into bed.

By this time Slippy, who was an adored wife at home and had never been on a trek like this, began to complain to me. She had no illusions left about mountain hiking. She told me what she thought, saying, "Believe me, I am going to long distance my husband in the morning and tell him to come right after me!"

Inwardly I was bursting; I thought if he should have a repetition of our difficulties on the trail, he would give up long before he got there. I thought, poor Slippy, she is a good egg and will feel a lot different by morning when she has had a good sleep.

Even with the hot rocks in bed, we had trouble in getting to sleep as we couldn't seem to get warm. We woke up every so often shivering and pulling the sweaters up. Every time we turned over, they seemed to be around our feet.

At last, with the distant cry of a coyote, and the winking firelight showing through the isinglass on the door of the little stove, we fell asleep.

I couldn't hear myself so I don't know if I snored, but judging by her snoring, Slippy was sure having a rough ride down that mountain.

In the small hours there was a terrific CRASH in the cabin! Slippy stayed dead to the world, but I was instantly on the *qui vive*. I held very still and listened and I thought, aha, a brush ape or something equally as bad! Nothing happened and, as the sun came to bring a new day, it was discovered that it had only been one of our nice hot rocks falling out of bed.

Morning was so delightful after the night before that we all thought in unison, it was the loveliest day of the year AND our clothes were dry. Anyone who has never eaten openfire flapjacks has missed one of the highlights of the open air revelry. These we washed down with cup after cup of plain boiled coffee made in the loggers' tradition.

Slippy now saw the world in a new light. After breakfast, we trailed down the mountain again, and on our way we got the first medical aid possible for the injured man. Morning—a shining glory as rosy hues caught the nearer peaks around us, and tumbled off to tinge each separate wild flower on the trail down.

We stopped again at the abandoned camp where we picked up some souvenirs. Mine was a large blue pitcher with Chinese birds on the side.

Slippy changed her mind on the way down about never wanting to go again!

In the spring months of 1942, Grace Gardner, editor of the mining bulletin "Monte Cristo Today" wrote:

"Monte Cristo, long drugged in a Rip Van Winkle sleep, shows healthy signs of bestirring itself, shaking its half century of tangled whiskers, blinking crow's feet eyes, and looking upon a brand new world, the blazed trail through the tall conifers for fifty years known as the Monte Cristo Trail, now is history;!"

5

Metaline

That fall I took an appointment at Metaline, Washington. Before leaving, I invested in a pair of glasses which I was supposed to need, but which I thought would give me a more sedate and dignified look.

I traveled by train from Seattle, going up on a branch line of the Milwaukee from Spokane. This town is located about twelve miles from the Canadian border in Pend Oreille County.

I had never been over this area and each new turn in the road was a revelation. A short distance out of Spokane the country began to be more hilly, and was covered with jack pines. As we passed into an ever higher elevation the timber became taller and of a more dense growth. The train followed the bed of the Pend Oreille River for miles, crossing deep canyons where the river rushed in swirling eddies, this all overhung by the shadowed green of the deep forest.

We passed through Newport, the county seat, on a hill overlooking the sweeping arc of the river. The Milwaukee Road swings in a westerly direction from Newport. We climbed for a few more miles and then turning north, wound along the east side of the river. This route is marked by a procession of logged off lands, forested hills and stump ranches. We crossed then through heavy forests of pine, tamarack and fir. Rising through the deep cleft of the river's channel were bench lands and a series of ascending terraces which broke into the steep and rugged mountain slopes.

We were in the area of the Kaniksu National Forest which extends in some places into Idaho.

We now passed over Box Canyon which is twelve thousand feet long and from twenty to one hundred feet in height. It is very hard to put in words that are not hackneyed the great beauty of this scenery.

We came out at last to the great forking of the river before it narrows and tumbles wickedly over the rocks in Dead Man's Eddy, then over Metaline Falls. Looking from the Metaline Falls side of the river, I saw what appeared to be a small village. This is often referred to as Old Town. This was my destination.

I was met at the train by the clerk of the school board and the lady with whom I was to stay. I felt anything but professional as the new glasses were too strong and were making me see double. (I took them off and have never worn any since.) We crossed the Metaline Falls bridge where we paid the toll that was levied at that time.

As we came down the main street of the town, it impressed me as a lonely Alaskan village might have. There were few buildings, only one of which was occupied. The only activity noted was the general store, which presented and old-fashioned facade, with a small, one-room post office hugging it. Farther down the street was an old dance hall, and an abandoned hotel. The street adjacent to this one bordered on the river bank, where there were several small cottages. The school consisted of two rooms and sat back on a slight rise away from the river.

The Burgan home where I stayed was small, cozy and very neat, situated on a large level lot bordering the river and, in the front yard, as well as the next two adjoining lots, was a grove of pine trees.

The other teacher and I were to occupy the front bedroom. But she had not arrived with me.

That evening during dinner, a red roadster was seen buzzing back and forth in front of the house and Mrs. Burgan told me these were the young bloods of the town and were probably anxious to get a glimpse of the teachers.

Having arrived the day before Labor Day, the children came around and invited me to go swimming with them. I went in with them the following day. The water was delightfully clean and clear and there was a raft anchored there from which we swam. The children were very happy because all their teachers before had not been too keen about the river, and were not swimming enthusiasts as I was.

The week-end after school started I decided to swim across the river. Everyone advised me against this, saying that I had no idea how very swift the current was out in the middle. There was a long sand bar out there where the river forked to go into its final plunge over Dead Man's Eddy.

I waded in up to my neck, then with easy strokes slowly and surely eased myself out into the current. I thought, if I could make it how thrilled I would be. When I got out into the main current I swam just as fast as I could so as not to be carried too far down the river. I would land on the sand bar in the middle of the river where the river forked.

When I thought my lungs would burst, the current began to lessen and I slowly came into shallower water and finally put my feet down on the sand bar.

I landed, breathing heavily, and gave the flyers' O.K. signal—my thumb touching the middle finger—and waving my arm violently to all the children and parents who had collected on the shore. This was a terrible strain on the town, I guess. They put their cupped hands over their mouths, calling to me, saying, "No, no don't do it; wait for a boat, don't try to come back!"

By this time they all were wishing that they had never seen me probably. We called back and forth for some time, no one being able to hear anyone else too clearly over the roaring surge of the river.

I thought: I just won't give up! Wouldn't that be a nice kettle of fish to be kidded all winter about the time they rowed the teacher back from the swim. It was 'do or die' so I waved back.

Several of the more chicken-hearted mothers covered their faces with their hands. It was a long long swim. After I had reached the swiftest part, I rolled over on my back and swam without my hands the rest of the way in. This gave my arms a rest and my lungs a chance to get caught up.

When I came close in to shore they were all yelling and laughing and giving hesitant credit. One lady fainted and it was some minutes before she ever quite forgave me all winter.

The next time I upset the town was when I went for a ride on "Whitey." Whitey was a gray horse that came down the mountain and browsed around occasionally. He had been given up by the young bloods of the town as being hard to handle. All the children were deathly afraid of him. (The Wild Stallion of Lost Gulch—Yes?) I got one of the boys to catch him and lead him up to the schoolhouse steps where I mounted him.

Our trip down the main street was high, wide, and not too pretty. Necks were craned out of upper story windows. Whitey and I, however, turned out to be kindred spirits. After I had stayed on for about fifteen minutes, he began to calm down and I brought him back down the street. Some of the smallest children followed, but when the horse came pretty close, one of them began to cry.

During the winter I went to several old-fashioned basket socials. There was always much merriment and conjecture over WHO would get the TEACHER'S BASKET. When there was a dance in town it took the women all the preceding afternoon to sweep out the town hall and get it ready.

I went on rides in the vicinity of Nelson, B.C. on week-ends. There were dances on the U.S. side of the line, that is just a stone's throw away. I went to one of these in the middle of the winter; it was very cold and the highway was covered with a sheet of ice. The trip around the mountain had to be taken in easy stages. We went in a foursome, the other teacher, a small, alert red-head was keen on diversions and the type that was ready for anything, and to me life at this point was a succeeding series of challenges. No challenge, no fun.

We were very cold coming down the mountain after one of these events. Our escorts stopped the car in front of a mountain cabin where an old Canadian friend of theirs lived. The boys urged us to come in and get warm. The snow at this point was about three feet deep.

Their Canadian asked us if we would take a 'toddy' if he would fix it for us. After some hesitation, we agreed as we were about fainting with the cold. He got out a little old teakettle and heated some water, poured in a small amount of liquor into each of two glasses and stirred in a piece of butter. This was our first experience with a Hot Butter Scotch. We felt a bit guilty but didn't have any trouble keeping our feet warm the rest of the way down the mountain. I have never tasted such a drink since; there must have been some mystery to the alchemy of this little old Canadian trapper!

There were rainy times, too. Sometimes it would be very wet and then freeze. One time we came home in a silver frost. This to a western novice would be a unique experience. A whole forest encased in glass. Now and then the crashing to the ground of a limb that had fallen with its encasement of ice, a benign moon hanging over all.

When we ran out of something to do we carried a portable phonograph on the shelf of a coupe, rode out into the forest where we enjoyed the music and society of someone who said, 'And do you love me, too?' This, however, before one could have had a radio equipped car.

Was this not a dream? The stillness of the sheltering forest, as only a forest can be still and the steady drip, drip, drip of the rain. If we ran out of needles we used a thorn gathered from bushes along the way.

6

Junior Jack Tars

At the outbreak of World War II, when teachers were in such demand, as a patriotic gesture I took a position in a private school for boys, the Puget Sound Naval Academy at Winslow, Washington. This school was conducted along naval lines; an Annapolis in miniature.

It was situated on Puget Sound, the entrance to the campus being about half a mile from the main road. The buildings consisted of two "Halls" and a large gymnasium.

During the first year that I was there, I was in the unit for smaller boys. I was in charge of these boys for all their subjects except sports, that is the regular athletics, and the naval drills which came at eleven o'clock.

This was a change from the public school program and in some ways there was more opportunity for new ideas to be carried out.

My free hour from eleven to twelve seemed a privilege, as I could go to my room and read until lunch time. There was always time to make myself tidy for lunch, as I could hear the bugles which always blew for the beginnings of each separate activity.

In the early evening after dinner, some of my pupils often came to my room during their free hour before study period. I played games such as checkers and parchesi with them. They often shared with me incidents of their home life and the things that they were especially interested in. There was one little Jewish boy that I was attracted to. He was good in music and often sang for me some of the chants he had learned in the synagogue. All this had to be done quietly so as not to disturb the study period of the older boys.

Sometimes after school on rainy nights, of which there were

plenty, I planned informal parties in my room for them. If they got a pass they could go to a store nearby for some goodies. They often ran all the way back and would come in breathless with wet coats and hats but just bubbling. I had a small electric plate and I made cocoa for them which I served with marshmallows.

My room was small for any group of children, and it was agreed between us that they could come only if they were very quiet. They learned to balance plates and cups on their knees, soon becoming past masters in the art.

One day I promised two different groups that they could come. They were to come in two different shifts due to the limited capacity of my quarters.

The first party arrived, thinking how they had hood-winked the others. Suddenly as they sat guiltily munching their food, a small noise was heard along the side of the building. (My quarters were on the corner of the building.) I opened a french window to see what was up. To my intense suprise, there was Grove climbing up the drain pipe. He was almost up to the window sill!

We pulled him in where he landed in an exhausted and giggling heap. We just gave up! I think he enjoyed the party twice as much because it was 'a steal.'

Other times I had the several women teachers for tea after school. This included the nurse and the Commandant's wife. My little bed did double duty with its load of teachers who considered themselves the cream of the crop. It was a trick showing considerable finesse to juggle and present an appetizing 'tea' in such a small space. All would remark afterward that they enjoyed this lots more than some of the real teas given by the school where all had to be so blah-blah!

It was pleasurable at the dinner hour to watch the boys line up for mess. There was some hilarity during the general assembling, but no monkey business after the first signal. When all were present and accounted for the salute would be given, and they marched in to dinner in good order.

If the boys did not pass inspection in the first line up, they were often sent back by the senior officer to be cleaned up. They would then have to go to the Commandant's table to make their excuses before sitting down."

One night when the faculty was having a formal buffet, one of the boys climbed up a fir tree overlooking the balcony of the sitting room where we were gathered. He wanted to see what the teachers were 'up to.' It was the same gremlin of the drainpipe episode.

It wasn't quite so funny to him, however, when he was summarily called before his superior officers when the weekly 'mast' was held and he got a flock of demerits!

I stayed on that year to teach in the summer school. We had only three major subjects for 'brush up' and there was no formal class work after eleven in the morning. At eleven the boys had their usual drill, then came lunch hour. The construction class was from one to two o'clock for the juniors. This was one of my classes.

Some of the things we made during the summer were miniature battleships, aircraft carriers and subs. The juniors loved this activity in which they were intensely interested. The rest of the afternoon was devoted to hiking, fishing and swimming. They fished every day and went hiking and swimming on the alternate days.

Conducting the junior swimming classes I enjoyed very much. They were very wiggly and full of pep and could hardly wait until the signal to go to the beach was given. First I gave them setting up exercises on the lawn in front of one of the Halls. They had put on their trunks and wore only their shoes, that is, until they reached the beach. Each boy carried his own towel.

At the signal they were allowed to dash down the winding path leading to the beach, but were to regain formation after they got down. All accounted for, we followed the shore line for about one fourth mile. Here was a fine sandy beach. The sand extended out for a distance of about three city blocks, the beach being clear of any debris.

Here they had full opportunity to display their swimming ability as well as other talents. They were delirious with happiness. They covered themselves and each other with sand, then they pretended they were commandos making a beachhead. I had to blow the whistle about fifteen minutes before they were due to start back in order to get them there in time. There were about thirty-five boys in this section.

Upon their arrival back, they were taken over by the coach, who kept them occupied until dinner time. Three-thirty would mark the end of this activity. I went then to my quarters and after a shower and a rub down, settled with a book for the rest of the afternoon. I wouldn't say that I never fell ASLEEP at these times.

At the beginning of the fall term, I took some of the more advanced boys. The Junior School was moved over into another building in order to give the senior section more room. Their baracks was on the third floor of the same building.

Along about the middle of the year, if the well known Ted Lewis had poked his head in the door and said, "Is everybody happy?" I wouldn't have answered "Yes" because I wasn't!

The Junior Head and I began to be on the 'outs.' This was caused by the partiality she had shown in the seating arrangements in the dining room.

She had a favorite with whom she wished to share her table. Formerly another teacher and myself had joined them. I had instructions that with the new arrangement, we two were to sit at other tables about the room.

It was first decided that I was to sit at Mr. M's table, the science and math teacher. He was an older man, very distinguished looking, and a pleasure to talk to.

When the Junior Head saw that I was so well pleased with this arrangement and we were getting along so toppingly, she didn't like it. She made the excuse that there was no one to sit at the far end of the room with the very youngest, called the "dypes" who had formerly had their matron sit with them. I was then banished to this ignominious task.

I stood it for several days then made up my mind that enough was enough. I wrote her a note telling her I hadn't been employed in the capacity of a nursemaid. I considered this beneath my dignity. It wouldn't have been so unfair except for the fact that they had had a nurse previously for these same boys, and now I was to act in that capacity during the meals!

My former seat having been at the head of the dining room, it was embarrassing to have to walk down the length of the dining room with all eyes upon me. It was the longest room I have ever walked down!

I also said in my note that if I couldn't have the seat back at Mr. M's table by the following day, that I would leave, which I summarily did.

It seemed a large thing then, but seems of little consequence now. Small things can be a bitter pill to swallow under a given set of circumstances.

About two weeks later, I received word from the school asking me to re-consider and return. It took a lot of courage but I did. The Junior Head was still there, I was seated at her table, but I will never forget that first meal.

I had additional duties and worked in the office part of the time. To do this we were naturally thrown together again. I was to do some of her letters for her. The understanding being that I would not have to take any dictation from her literally or figuratively.

The first few days she wrote me notes of instruction regarding her letters. When she saw the glint of a weakening ire in my eyes, and that after all I seemed to bear her no ill will, she warmed up some.

And I think that in her heart she realized that we had both been very foolish.

After I had been back a while, for various reasons I began to feel sorry for her. I had been put in charge of ordering some of the supplies for the school and employing some of the kitchen and dining room help. She was nonplussed when she saw that I was given so much authority. I managed, however, to make things agreeable for her and she had to like me in spite of herself. I hope if she reads this she will forgive me as she was a valiant soul in ways that are not gauged by material things.

When she went away one week-end I planned a little surprise for her. One of the new employees had usurped the use of one of her rooms, and I really did feel sorry about that. I found a room in one of the Halls that I knew she would just love if it were fixed up.

I had the housekeeper clean it out and hang fresh drapes. I arranged to have a desk put in there, comfortable chairs, and all the things I thought she'd like. I ordered some flowers from town. First I was going to have cut flowers then thought a potted plant would be preferable and last longer.

When she came back from the city I told her that there was a surprise for her and that the housekeeper would show her what I meant. She was quite overcome; she was not a person to make a vulgar display of her feelings, but I know that she really appreciated this gesture—she and I lived happily ever after.

Around graduation time, I received an offer from the Washington State School for Boys at Chehalis, Washington, which offered me a much higher salary. This school at that time was in session for twelve months. I told them that I would be unable to come for at least a month. In the interim my employer raised his own figure. We had lots of fun and joking over the deal, but he said, "Well, after all, you can't expect a private operator to compete in salary with a state organization."

He was a very fine man, I always liked him and always will. One reason that I liked him was that he could always see the funny side of things. He was always laughing and ready for a joke. I kept some of the accounts for him (at which I was rather green) but he helped me and we had lots of fun together.

My father got a bang out of it when he heard I had been given the combination of the safe. He said, "I don't know if he was wise in trusting you, you know you are rather handy 'with the chips.'"

The two of them would have made a great pair!

I played the piano for graduation. The piece "Anchors Aweigh" was appropriate for me, too, as it also was my leave taking.

This was a very solemn occasion and one that I shall always cherish in retrospect. There can be nothing to equal the feeling one gets in sharing other people's lives in this intimate way. (And then there are some people who say they would not be a teacher for anything in the world.) It will always be touching sending youth on to their future.

I felt for them a kindred feeling of 'leave taking.'

"The ship of life whereon we sail
Has many ports, they say;
One of them you are leaving now,
This graduation day."

I would always have the remembrance of the boys out on the drill field, the well clipped commands; the hurry and the bustle that accompanied the getting ready for the month ends at home; the gay camaraderie between them after school; the barking of the mascot; the pre-emptory calls of the coach's whistle to make them hurry through their showers, and lastly, the inherent pride shining in the eyes of each individual parent on this their graduation day!

7
Boys' Limbo

I had an interesting time when I went to the Washington State Training School for Boys at Chehalis, Washington to be interviewed. I had arrived shortly after noon. I was ushered into a large office and greeted by the superintendent, a rather rotund man possessing clear blue eyes, a straight from the shoulder manner and a quick, businesslike movement. I was also introduced to the principal of the academic part of the school and the assistant superintendent.

The principal had rather prominent teeth, a ready smile and appeared to be a fatherly sort of person. His assistant had an odd unpredictable smile. As I sat there I wondered what my associations with these varied personalities would be.

We all talked together for a few minutes in a jovial way. The superintendent made some general remarks about the school, making some reference to the new administration building that was being planned. There was a large roll of blueprint on his desk. These he said were the plans for all the new construction and that the delay was in waiting for the State Legislature to make the appropriation.

After the three months wait for the conclusion of my duties at the naval school, I arrived late one Sunday afternoon. The principal came to the depot to meet me. Arriving at my dormitory, I was shown to my quarters and told that supper would be served in the employees dining room in about an hour.

I looked about me to find a neat but severe looking room. There were glass curtains over the two windows that overlooked a beautiful garden. (At that moment I made a mental picture of the drapes I would put up later, that could be pushed back to give a clear view of the garden, and drawn without the use of old-fashioned shades at night.) There was a plain, meticulously clean bed, a small desk, a straight chair, and a large, heavy, handmade rocker in the seat of which there was a pillow covered with cross barred blue and white material, which I assumed had probably been made there in the workshop.

I sat down for a few minutes to collect my thoughts before starting to unpack. I noticed immediately under the window sill, a large iron ring into which was drawn a heavy rope almost as thick as a steamboat hauser. I wondered what this was for, my vivid imagination pictured boys being ited up with it and perhaps punished. That together with the BARRED material for the pillow, gave me an errie feeling.

As I sat there I listened. No sound broke the stillness of this late Sunday afternoon.

I got to my feet and began to unpack one of my suitacses. I had a very lonely feeling as this place seemed to present a quiet tomblike atmosphere, compared to the gentle bustle and general activity of a Sunday afternoon at the Naval School.

Presently I began to wonder why there was no one special to break out the welcome mat, after my coming from so far away. I didn't exactly expect a brass band, but the greeting of at least one woman would have been pleasant.

Now I heard a piercing, all-consuming whistle blowing; it sounded to me like the whistle men must hear after a hard day at the salt mines. This I had been told would be my signal to go to supper.

I examined my countenance in the mirror and made a final adjustment to my dress, and ran a comb through my hair and thought to myself: 'If you have any personality, kiddo, you had better start shining.' Then I walked slowly out of the room and down two flights of stairs to the ground level going over to the building in which I was told I would find the dining room.

I entered a cool tile entranceway from which came enticing smells. There was no one in the dining room at this time, except the attendants who were all in immaculate white. I waited. The people began to straggle in in two's and three's, talking volubly, but paying no attention whatever to me. I felt then like a riderless horse wandering in an abandoned town at dusk.

Soon the signal was given and the glass doors going in to the dining room were opened and we all went in. One of the men ushered me to a designated table, showing me my place and telling me that that was where I would eat all of my meals.

I was introduced to the people at the table. I found it rather hard to make conversation. I was stared at with the so-this-is-the NEW-

ONION-that-has-been-planted-in-our-garden look. I afterwards thought maybe if I would appear each day in some new attire, perhaps it would not seem to have too-freshly-peeled a look. Being ogled was one thing and doing a little of the same in my own interests was another.

I could soon see that this was no one's frolic, BUT having had the onion experience before, I felt that I was as interesting to them perhaps as they were to me.

The supper was very good. A well-balanced meal, and every appointment of the table was most sanitary and immaculate to the nth degree.

Each table in the room was centered with a bouquet of freshly cut flowers (from the hot-house, I was told). Today's flowers were sweet peas. The delicious home-like order of the flowers merged with the smell of fresh linen and the food. As I gazed about the room at the bouquets at each table, my mind went back to Mother's special planting of sweet peas that she had planted with such regularity each spring. That remembrance helped me in getting over my singular greeting here.

As I had come down the walk approaching the dining rooms, I heard the tramp of many marching feet. I saw the boys walking two by two and being counted off as they passed in to their dining room.

Now as I came out, there was a marked stillness and I learned that the boys had preceded us in coming out. They were now finishing some special duties or engaged in sports. I forgot to mention that all the attendants in the dining room were older boys who had earned enough merits to be 'on trust,' that is, all the attendants with the exception of the head dietician and kitchen helpers.

I walked then slowly back to my quarters, enjoying the gardens as I went. I unpacked the rest of my belongings and settled my room as near to my taste as I could. There was the problem of moving the bed around to a more artistic corner. Then there was that heavy rocker. I tried to pick it up but it was no go. I couldn't lift it. Finally I managed to ease it up against the bed, and rolling it over the bed to get it on the other side of the room. (After I was there awhile, I succeeded in painting it ivory, and putting a splashy cover on the pillow.)

I was still stuck on the rope and the ring. My fertile brain began to take me back to possible early days in the institution when they might have had use for it. I imagined they might have tied boys up with it. My curiosity was satisfied when I was later told that this rope had been used as a fire escape in the early days when the building had been new. They had never bothered to have it removed. My flight of fancy came down then with a soft 'plop' and I felt more at home from then on.

The following morning I was to start my duties. Breakfast was at seven-thirty A.M. This was a meal at which no one did very much talking. The floors here were scrubbed down with hot water and soap EVERY MORNING by the 'house detail,' and woe betide the adult that tried to procrastinate by being too long winded in the dining room. I soon learned why there wasn't too much time for sociability in the accepted sense. This was precision movement personified.

I came then with the other teachers, to the line up for classes; the boys marching into the school building two by two. The teacher I was superceding was there that morning to give me pointers in the general plan of the teaching day there. I had the seventh grade in the morning and the eighth grade in the afternoon.

There were many little things I would have to learn about a school of this kind. The boys were not allowed to go to the lavatory unaccompanied, unless they were top merit boys and due to be released soon. The usual recesses were allowed, but the boys were limited to a very small playground and were observed all during their playtime both by their teachers and a company manager.

That first morning I was there, two boys slipped away. They ran down into an adjoining cow pasture where they were soon caught. These boys were referred to as 'ramblers' and had all of their merits taken away, this made 'time' start all over for them. Following this event, high wire fences were put up around this same quadrangle.

The following morning I saw the two runaways. Their hair had been shaved off, and their shoes taken away; they were wearing house slippers. They were very young and I felt sorry for them. (It wasn't hard for me to be sorry for them, having come so recently from a school where the indulgent parents paid many guilders just for tuition!)—Some contrast.

Other punishments for these ramblers who were looked down upon, was having to 'stand out' during the recess period when the other boys were playing. They had to stand on a certain spot not moving, not talking to the other boys.

They attended school only four hours a day, spending the rest of the time on their work details. They were assigned to some work in which they were interested, except for the smaller boys, who could not choose their own, or for neurotics or any other boys having no special talents. All the left over boys served on the 'house detail' and were taught general housekeeping, the cleaning angle especially. They worked in crews usually of from eight to ten boys under a sort of house mother.

The teachers' rooms were kept in immaculate condition by these crews, the linens and etc. being changed at very frequent intervals.

The principal of the elementary department told me at the beginning of my work there not to be too disappointed if my pupils did not make the customary progress made in mublic schools. Some, he said, were retarded for many and varied reasons, some with pronounced maladjustments. This I soon found out.

Some would take only a certain amount of serious study, so that part of their instruction period I would spend in reading to them. This school was different in that there was a wide variance and divergence in their capacities, so that it was verging on the impossible, in some cases for them to keep pace, and recite together even though they were in the same class. This was the numbing effect for the teacher. At that time two kinds of remedial rooms were needed, but not enough money had been given by the State Legislature for this purpose.

It was very hard each afternoon after school for me to become used to the quietness that would prevail. (Our teaching day ended at four forty-five P.M.) Especially after the supper hour. A beautiful garden to look out on; the flag blowing stiffly in the breeze, but no sound of laughter, running feet, and a barking mascot, as there had been at the Naval School.

This was hard indeed to become accustomed to. I couldn't help but think of how endless the long evenings must be for the boys confined after supper to their Company rooms. (They were divided into companies according to age. There would be from fifty to seventy-five in each company, this number varying some with the constantly changing enrollment.)

Due to war time conditions—W.W. II the first part of my time there—there was no athletic instructor. So this part was left out entirely except for occasional trips to the gym during the week and on Saturday mornings. Later, however, the school was successful in getting a very fine athletic instructor who had prepared men for the army. Then the boys had forty-five minutes for gym two or three days a week.

As these periods came due, each teacher escorted his group to the gym where the boys would be counted in. There were two other women teachers besides myself.

One of the company managers I detested for no apparent reason, except that he had a very supercilious manner. The period of which I speak was during the late fall, winter, and before the advent of spring. He wore a long grey overcoat, well buttoned up. His had was usually slid at a precarious angle over his eyes. He gave the impression that nothing could be done right unless he was on the spot. He was the type that would have gloried in being the person to make the major address of the evening at a grave diggers' ball, he didn't have the aura of friendliness protrayed by Digger O'Dell and his ilk. I called him 'Lord Chesterfield' behind his back, although I knew the real Chesterfield belonged to a different strata of society. Well, anyway, he just HAD to be LORD somebody!

One particular day I was escorting my group over to the gym. A Company manager usually followed behind any group being moved. Instead of bringing up the rear as was customary, he met my group at the turn, leading and walking just as slow as he possibly could. He probably had been instructed from the superintendent to slow the group up some, but he made it EXTRA SLOW just to show his authority. I felt quite chagrined. By doing this he gave me a feeling of inadequacy, and incapability of the proper dispatch of my duties.

He did this for several days. Came another day. I thought I would play a trick on him. My group came to that special turn. There stood Lord Chesterfield, standing, waiting in all his pomposity; I had taken the lead of my group myself, leaving HIM to bring up the rear. I walked as fast as I could. This necessitated his walking faster to keep up.

I had told some of the other teachers what I was going to do. It was arranged that they glance idly out their windows as we went by. They agreed later that it was the funniest thing they had ever seen. For once, they saw Lord Chesterfield on the double, which shot quite an arrow into the blimp of his self-complacency. They said afterwards that all we would have needed was a flag and a drum.

The athletic instructor met me at the entrance to the gym. I told him what I had done, and as his Lordship rounded the bend, the instructor had all he could do to hold in, as he nonchalantly, if surreptitiously was peering at his stop watch held in the palm of his hand.

The boys weren't allowed to have anything of value to keep, or anything of a personal nature. They were hungry, too, for a touch of home. As is a habit with any group of children, they noticed the clothes the teachers wore. We could tell by little ways in which they talked together about the slightest thing that was different, so-and-so's new shoes or dress, etc. There were a few minutes each day when they were allowed to come to the desk for informal conversation, that is if they had been quiet during the reading period. I had an old coat pin with three small pendants on a chair. I didn't know about this rule and I told one of the boys he could have it to heep as long as he had admired it so much.

He wore it proudly on his sweater for a couple of days. One of the days following during inspection one of the meaner managers noticed it. He asked the boy where he got it. The lad told him. The man took it off him and threw it in the ash-can. The rest of the boys were quite incensed about this.

The principal of the school got wind of it, and he and the Company manager had an argument over it. The principal told him in no uncertain terms what he thought of him. He told him that if he didn't want the boy to have it, the least he could have done would have been to return it to me. The boy in question was a sad looking little fellow, with a hang dog expression, who perhaps had never had any kindness or personal attention in his life. I felt rather sick about it at the time and was sorry that I had caused so much trouble for all concerned; if you could see the expression in the eyes of some of those boys, you would feel more than a tug at your heartstrings; you would never forget it as long as you lived.

The only music that the boys had was when they had church services on Sundays, or an occasional movie would be shown. As I have previously noted, I am very fond of music. There was no piano available to the boys nor the teachers, the only pianos in rooms open to the public were in the auditorium, and one of the reception parlors in the administration building. (Last noted would never be played as it was too adjacent to the cold room where parents had to bid farewell to their boys, or some boy waited perhaps for a father who had 'promised' for the visiting day, but did not sometimes show up.) I forgot to mention a piano I recall now in one of the Company rooms that wasn't allowed to be played, I suppose because of the inadequacy in musical ability of the general run of the boys, and the fact that I suppose it would have created some argument between the boys, or make too much noise at inopportune times.

I told the boys that if I could get the key for the auditorium, that I would play for them, and they would be able to listen from their barracks on the floor below. I managed to get the key and the permission to use the piano in the auditorium, but I said nothing about wanting to play for the boys, as I thought it was taboo and might get them in trouble some way.

I went in, It was all dark with blackout curtains (war time) and had the unused smell of all closed places as it was only opened at weekly intervals. I didn't know where any of the light switches were and so I had to experiment. I finally found, in this dungeon-like place, the switch controlling the light over the piano. There was no bench nor stool. I fluttered around looking for a chair or something that I could sit on; I hadn't found the master switch and so most of this place was in semidarkness except for the light over the piano. All that I could find was a small one that was much too low. I got hold of a bunch of hymnals and piled them up to make a seat high enough. Success at last!

I played for over two hours until I knew the boys would have to go to bed. By that time the perspiration was running down my back, but I inwardly exulted because I thought all the time of how they would be enjoying it.

Next morning I thought when we had our conversational period, the boys would be telling me about how they had enjoyed the music, but all morning an unusual silence seemed to pervade my classroom; not a word was said so I finally asked them if they hadn't heard me. They said, "No." I was much non-plussed to learn that the floor was soundproof.

Endlessly the days rolled forward, no particular day being much different than any other except when something out of the general routine occurred. I went in to the small town near there about twice a week for dinner and a show. It was relaxing to get off "the hill" at these times.

Days in the early spring our school had baseball in competition with the other schools in nearby towns. On these days if the women teachers did not wish to witness the games they got off duty earlier.

I planned a vacation in June to which I was entitled after having been inresidence eleven months. By the time my vacation time did materialize, however, I had been there for fourteen months.

I had decided that I would not plan on staying into the second year, after my return. Also the governorship of the state was changing, and none of us were too sure of our places for political reasons. I had had a pretty good offer elsewhere.

That fall I planned taking a position offered me in Oregon. The man holding the principalship had been a teaching fellow with me at the Naval School.

No leave taking is ever carried out without some pangs. I had succeeded in making many friends while here. I had a small gathering in my quarters the day I left, at which we had a chance to bid hail and farewell.

I could not help but think of what had transpired here; I learned many things I otherwise might not have known. There had been some shining hours, that God had given me because I had given of myself, and there were some days cast in shadow, but I would not soon forget the happy days.

It was wonderful to have had the experience, even if an experience here over a period of years would have been stagnating (due to the endless pattern the program followed and the lack of studious interest by the larger percent of the boys).

I can still see the shining happy eyes of the waif to whom I gave the pin, and I hope that if he reads my book, or chances upon it in the future in his manhood, that he will remember me. The greatest acclaim to any teacher is in being remembered.

I thought of these things as I drove down the long avenue of trees that marked the entry to the grounds. It would have been a pleasure to have indulged in a fairy story where all the wrong things would have been righted and the boys turned out, as off an assembly line 'just like new.'

8

Continental Skyways

       The Dream today,
       To whir away
       On the wings of a Silver Ship!

I had come a long way since that long ago day when I had slipped away and out of the house at Park Point to go to the Aerial Bridge at Duluth.

Perhaps it wasn't just because I loved my Father and wanted to follow him.

In my unformed mind I knew instinctively that there was something new 'out at the bridge.'

I looked down and without realizing that an impression was being made, I stared at the churning water beneath the bridge; then turning my small self I looked out to the far end of the Point and the lighthouse.

I saw the far horizon line that I was too young to understand.

I wondered what happened at the place where the water and sky were buttoned together so neatly.

Did I think of this really, or was it the magnet of my natural illusiveness of spirit that drew me on to the discovery of an ever-widening world?

In my childhood I had flown with "The Little Lame Prince" in his magic cloak. Now, I would fly today to find out what REALLY was at 'the buttoning place.'

Books, yes, my whole world had been books, but to know reality was to BE THERE!

I wanted, myself, to unbutton corners of America.

I believed in My America as I had believed in the wisp of silk that was My Flag, stuck in the ivy of a Canadian landed estate on the Dominion Day so many years ago.

Now, I would see for myself!

*   *   *

I went down to Boeing Field the morning of my departure at a little before eight A.M. My plane, a DC 6, was due to leave at eight-thirty.

My friend Adelaide had come down to see me off.

We had coffee together in the Sky Room, while awaiting the departure time. She had brought me a delicious box of homemade cookies.

My first trip on the DC 6!

My seat was rather far back as I always wanted the starboard tail seat, or as far back as I could get.

We were down in about an hour or less at the Spokane field. There was considerable waiting here for another plane that was supposed to make the Minneapolis connection. We were all given gate passes so that we could get out for the duration of the wait.

It was a clear day and there was much activity on the field with the planes constantly arriving and departing. _____ Field was an interesting place. In the lobby was a large stone fireplace. The room was finished in knotty pine which gave a homelike touch. The lunchroom and commissary were located in an adjoining building. I went over there to pick up some magazines. It was fun at a time like this to mosey around and study the people.

I met a very nice elderly woman who was going to visit her daughter in Minneapolis. She had a young girl with her, about eleven years old. I asked her if the child was her granddaughter and she said, "Oh no, I just met her on the plane and so we are making friends."

It proved that the girl had one parent in Seattle and the other in New York. She was going to New York for the summer. She happened also to be on one of the Quiz Kid programs. She was very intelligent and refreshing to talk to.

The lady and the young girl were great pals on the trip.

We finally got off the field at Spokane, flying at approximately twelve thousand feet, non-stop to Minneapolis.

White clouds rolled in knotty bunches beneath us. The Montana mountains had very little snow on them at this time of year and were not clearly visible, the tops of them being enfolded in the clouds.

We spun along at a steady pace and the monotonous hum of the four motors made me sleepy.

I spent part of the time up in the forward section of the ship, talking to my two friends.

Our Quiz Kid had her dolls well distributed up in the corner. They were seated in the last seat forward, adjacent to the flight deck. A child that knew all the answers, she seemed out of place with the dolls, they didn't seem to belong together.

Presently, as we were now riding in a white nowhere, I returned to my seat to read. As I looked from my seat down the aisle to the forward section, it seemed hard to realize that this was not a modern train.

That is one of the things about the larger planes that I don't like. There is more of a sense of adventure in riding the smaller planes; you get the feel of the ship more; the smaller ships (I thought at this point) have more personality.

Now we were over the wheat fields of North Dakota, with the granaries and small towns here and there. It seemed to me to be a gently rolling terrain—at least it seemed so with the speed we were traveling.

Time seemed to be escaping as sand would through a sieve. Now we were over the State of Minnesota, and the land of ten thousand lakes.*

It is rather hard to express the reaction I got as I looked down to this fertile country of smaller farms; then the forests with the prisms of small lakes set on a carpet of lush green. The lakes were child sized mirrors set on a green plush landscape.

The size of some of the lakes had been augmented by melting snows in the more mountainous areas.

Minneapolis

We approached the field at Minneapolis at around six P.M., having added two hours, changing our watches for the difference in the time belts. The actual non-stop flight was six hours.

The last part of this first lap of my journey was spoiled for me by anxiety over transfer connections going to Duluth. As events turned out I missed it by fifteen minutes.

One of the first things I noticed on my arrival here in Minneapolis was that the travel clerks at this airport were working with their coats off. It was very very warm.

There was considerable hub-bub and confusion. Long lines of people were waiting before the various windows for service on their tickets and connections.

*By actual count there are over eleven thousand lakes.

Each clerk was answering two phones at a time. They were all perspiring profusely.

I joined one of the queues.

It was rather hard to keep calm as I didn't know at that time if I would make the Duluth connection.

At last, my turn!

I was advised that I had missed it and that there was no other plane out of Minneapolis for Duluth till morning.

The clerk was very accommodating, however, and told me that he would make hotel arrangements for me. I said, "Call the best hotel and work down the list."

After some minutes, he told me he had accommodations at The Dykeman for me. He then checked the morning flight to Duluth for me. With a grateful heart, I went over to the baggage counter.

I got into a cab for downtown Minneapolis. I wasn't physically tired but the thing that drags on a long trip is the worry over connections along the way. I didn't notice whether I took the regular Limousine service, I just got in to the first available cab. A half hour run and I was in Minneapolis.

Approaching the central part of town, we passed down a street of once beautiful homes that were now being used as business establishments (from insurance offices to mortuaries). Nothing could take away the charm, however, of the tree shaded avenues with wide parking strips and well kept up lawns.

There was an incongruity here—the two did not seem to go together.

Now we were in front of the Dykeman. I didn't see the entrance and was craning my neck to find it. I said to the cabby, "Where's the hotel?"

He countered with, "It isn't across the street, lady!"

I thought, you nasty man, you aren't a very good greeter for your city.

I expected a good stiff cab fare. I was surprised to learn that it was only eighty-six cents. I couldn't imagine why he wanted the extra penny, as to my knowledge in Washington the cab fares are not taxed individually.

I was so agreeably surprised that I let him keep the change. IThis nearly killed me after his sarcasm, but I was game.)

The room finally!

I then discovered that I was hungry; I had spent an extra hour at the field waiting in line getting matters adjusted.

I changed, slicked up my hair, and went down to see what the possibilities foodward were. Now it was about eight P.M., Minneapolis time.

I inquired for the dining room, asking if they were still serving. The room was pointed out and I went in. I found that I was in the famous Robin Hood Room (but I wasn't feeling any too Robin-Hoody!).

I looked at the bill of fare and found that I could have most any kind of a DRINK that I wanted; the food seemingly was a side issue.

The menu read: Side Car, Half-n-Half, Mint Julep, Manhattan, etc.

Not being honestly what could be called a drinking woman, I thought: 'Why not? I am tired and might need it.'

I settled for a Russian Salad (how could I?), Port wine, and a rum-cherry sundae.

The waitress brought the wine first, and I thought I had nothing to lose, so I drank it.

I was just lifting the caviar off the 'Molotov' when the flood lights and floor show went on. This was a little more than I bargained for, but due to my propensities for the lighter side of life, I just didn't need a shove.

Then a gentleman approached my table and asked me to dance. I was feeling sort of, well, you know—so I accepted. We swung off into "I Ain't In The Mood For Love." (I just imagined that he was my father when HE was young.)

Other selections were: "I Don't Know Why I Love You Like I Do" and "Heartache." (About this time I was having them, being so far from home and my own William Powell.)

There was a very good whistler, Don Hennesy, who whistled, "Stumbling" and "Tico-Tico." If there had been any voting mine would have all gone to Hennesy, he was very very clever, and I hope he sees this!

The only thing I don't like about this sort of place is that the lights are so low you can't be sure of the cleanliness of the table appointments.

After we swung off into the second number, however, the table cloth became a minor issue.

Dinner over, I made my adieux, and so up to bed.

I thought I rather liked Minneapolis, even though my stopover there had been unplanned.

I arose at about six A.M. as my plane would leave the city early, and I wanted to have plenty of time.

I decided that I would go down the street and find the Radisson Hotel, and have breakfast there. (This was where I had wanted to stay in the first place.) It was only about two blocks away and I enjoyed a delicious breakfast.

The regular limousine service to the field would be leaving from in front of the Radisson, so I went back over to the Dykeman and packed up.

I stood out in front for some time while the doorman tried to hail a cab for me. We weren't having very good luck and I began to be worried that I wouldn't make it in time.

As luck would have it, I had forgotten my reefer and the bellhop went back after it.

We arrived at the Radisson just in time.

Duluth

On arriving at the airport, there was some little waiting to do after checking in at the desk. At about nine-thirty the plane for Duluth came in. Sailing off, the plane was a "daytime star" flashing back the sun's rays.

The trip from Minneapolis to Duluth was of short duration, the same being about an hour's run.

The land was caught in a series of what looked like hillocks but were much larger. Again there was the crystal sparkle of small lakes. I could see the land ahead for miles. It was an interesting home-like area. If I had been an artist getting motifs for the home scenes on Christmas cards, I would have been able to make a new picture as fast as I could draw.

As we were approaching Duluth, I flounced about in some of the vacant seats, trying to catch my first glimpse of Lake Superior from the air.

We came in rather slowly. I was a little disappointed as we came over the part of the lake nearest the city as it seemed to have a brownish tinge. Now we were flying over what once had been the Aerial Bridge of my very first runaway in that distant and entrancing past. Now it was a stationary all steel structure!

As we coasted within range of the depot on the ground, I saw two Sisters. I knew they were waiting for me and it made me feel important.

There was Sister Gerard! I had been a little worried about finding her and I didn't know whether she would be at St. Mary's Hospital or the College of St. Scholastica.

It was a wonderful surprise being met at the field.

I had sent Sister Gerard a wire from Minneapolis, and she had every minute planned for me, as I was to return to Minneapolis late the same afternoon.

We motored in to Duluth and up to the hospital. I was shown to a private sitting room on the third floor where I rested and made myself presentable. The little Sister who brought me up stairs was all smiles and happy camaraderie.

After a short visit, we went downstairs to Sister's private dining room where luncheon was served. No French chef could have cooked a better one! (A French Sister, I suppose.)

In the afternoon we went for a drive, driving first out to Park Point, and by the house where I was born. (This Point the scene of barefoot walk of Clifton and I so many years ago.)

The atmosphere was excatly the same as I had remembered it, except that the pines were fewer. The same Lake Superior bounding choppily around the point, the lighthouse, cottages and a substantial looking log cabin in the farther distance.

Surprisingly, the area was not too commercialized.

Wouldn't it be a dream to move into that log cabin or was it just a fairy story for me?

Some day I would come back and buy it!

We came back then into the city, motoring out to the main shoreline of Lake Superior. This superb lake!

We followed the Lake Shore "Skyline Drive" (the highway down the lake) for a distance of about thirty miles. This magic shore that had held so much of mystery to the early traders, Indians, and *couriers du bois* of a long gone time.

It was hard in the mind's eye to picture this scene as it must have appeared in those days. I knew the part my French forbears had played in this wild game with nature. Perhaps that is why I had fortitude and a never-say-die feeling for anything I undertook. Father often encouraged me when the going became a bit rough, he said, "You know, Marion, our people never gave up when the going became hard, they always went on to the fulfillment of their objectives."

One could look at this now benign land, with its surrounding blue of mighty waterway, picturing mentally the days of travail there must have been for the founding of even a small colony of homes in a savage land.

It was a mystery ever new to me. This land, in a sense, belonged to me as I did to it. One does not tear down in a moment of sliding by on fast modern feet, the memory of pioneer lands as they had once been; of the sorrows, heartaches, waiting, building, hoping and praying that had gone to the fulfillment of its well-ordered destiny.

We went then to the College of St. Scholastica, which is situated on a high hill overlooking Lake Superior.

From the exterior, which is built of St. Cloud granite and Bedford stone, the college looks like a medieval castle with all its battlements. Tower Hall is of English Tudor design, and the new buildings, are early Romanesque with turrets to conform with those of Tower Hall.

I was shown all through this remarkable edifice.

We entered a side door and walked down the length of the indoor portico, connecting two of the buildings. The chapel of Our Lady Queen of Peace is done in Early Romanesque style. It is one of the finest I have seen. The glass paintings of the chapel windows develops a theme in keeping with the dedication of the building.

The great east window of the facade represents in majestic figure, Our Lady Queen of Peace. Grouped around her, in figure and symbol, are those persons and institutions which are the harbingers of peace to mankind. The seventeen major windows of the aisles enter into the development of the peace theme. They represent seventeen young women saints whose lives and achievements made them instruments of peace in the world of their day.

We then passed through the various parlors, the floors of which are Kesota marble and Moos Lake tile in various colors. All the stone having been quarried in Minnesota.

The floors were waxed until they shone.

The right lobby parlor contained a chaise longue of Louis XIV style, and two low chairs of maple wood with hand made tapestry.

In the Sheraton dining room were closets containing the finest of china and figurines.

The floor of the Gold Parlor was covered with a Gorovan oriental rug. The settee and chairs were Out-back Empire, decorated with genuine bronze plate. They were imported original pieces, having the original tapestry which is at least ninety years old. The pattern was faded but was restored, brought out in oil painting by the Art department of the College.

There was an Oriental Parlor containing furniture of carved teakwood and ebony.

On the way down the stone stairway in front of the college, I looked off to the gently rolling hills of suburban Duluth.

I thought: what a privilege for any girl to attend college in this lovely place. If they could appreciate it just half as much as I did that there would be a certain joy in their college life that they could never forget.

We arrived back at the Duluth airport in time for me to make my connection back to Minneapolis again. At Minneapolis I would enplane again for Detroit.

Sister Gerald waited with me, and as the time for the leave-taking approached, it was hard for me to put my mind on commonplace things.

Our meeting was far from commonplace. I had often been intrigued watching meetings and departures of other people with Sisters who were dear to them. This is MY TURN. MY TURN!

The memory of it would never leave me. We had given each other mutually friendship and happiness.

As we stood arm in arm, I blinked away the tears rapidly. We were beloved friends. We would part again, each going toward the fulfillment of our separate destinies.

Sister Gerard watched the ship until it was out of sight.

Following this adventure I spent several days in Detroit, renewing some old friendships; then my sojourn ended as all good things must. I was reluctant to leave.

Detroit had been the scene for the early pioneer and fur trading endeavors of my French forbears. There is a street here named after one of them: Joseph Campau Avenue.

Witnessing the turbulence of this metropolis, it was hard to believe that thick forests had covered this land, where roamed at will the sloe-eyed deer and small wood animals that helped in their way to build this city into the metropolis it now was.

Could I rid myself of the nostalgia for this city of my forbears? Yes, I could go on; there would always be the store of memories that gave greater appreciation for everything in the Detroit that I was leaving!

I would have liked to slip back, if only for a moment, to walk up the trail, shoulder to shoulder, with any one of them, Jean Baptiste or Louis Campau.

One had been granted a piece of land on St. Anne and St. Antoine streets (within the stockade). 'Monsieur Campau' was to pay an annual rent of five *livres* and five *sous*; for the right to trade, ten additional *livres*. The rents were payable in furs or 'silver money when there would be any'. . .

I could drift back, living in imagination this long past time!

There was something left! It was not the stone, concrete and marble that had gone to build up this city, or any city, the thing that was left was the flesh, bone and sinew of those who followed after in all our land. THE PEOPLE who make a great world of today, and those who will make a great tomorrow!

Sailing along, again aloft, I could only think of 'blue skies smilin' at me, nothin' but blue skies do I see'. . . . A mechanical bird, yes, but if God didn't want man to fly he would never have made the part of man that makes such things possible.

9
Oregon Trails

The Coast Range and all the Tillamook country was a surprise to me. I traveled through a long winding maze of mountains wearing a coat of green in varying hues, each looking fresher and greener than the last; reaching the ridge and highest point, however, was not too pleasant an awakening, on the seaward side I looked down upon the areas that had once been acres and acres of fine forest land. Only tall blackened dead heads, a scrubby undergrowth at its feet scrawled across this terrain, as a reminder of the once beautiful forest that had covered this area.

There had been a great fire that in 1935 had destroyed one fourth million acres of Douglas Fir in less than twenty-four hours and other burns of less intensity. The whole forest at this point is a natural lure for the God of Fire. The winds blowing in from the ocean offer a perfect draft and there is nothing to stop the fanning of the flames.

Rolling down from the greater heights, I came to Turner's the stopping point for busses going between ocean points and Portland. The interior of this place was finished in knotty pine, the main room has a fireplace and at the time I was there two darling cocker spaniel puppies.

Going still farther down, I came now to the flatter land stretching away to the sea. I arrived at last at Nehalem.

One main street paralleled the river. Facing the river was a series of nondescript small shops with a post office sandwiched in between. From one side of the street I got a view of the river mouth as it flowed out to the sea, its waters darkened by the last sentinels of the Coast Range.

The principal met me. He had tried to get me a place to live but due to the fact that the fishing and tourist season was still on, there was nothing to be had. It was suggested that I bunk with one of the other teachers for the first night at least, until some arrangement could be made, but I did not favor the idea.

As we were discussing the matter, there came a heavy downpour of rain, accompanied by thunder and lightning. We stopped various places looking for accommodations but to no avail. I began to feel that if I could just be hung on a hook I would at least be out of the way!

As a last resort, the principal phoned one of the main homes of the town, explaining that there just wasn't any place for the teacher to stay, so the lady agreed to keep me until I would be able to find another place; she had taken people occasionally for short periods.

The house was large, square and old-fashioned but had been remodeled, having now all the latest features. The interior was done in exquisite taste, and was indescribably clean. This was better than anything I could have wished for in my fondest dreams and to top it off they were the kindliest and most charming people I had ever met.

I stayed there for the first month until I was successful in getting an apartment. This, however, was ten miles down the beach at Rockaway; it was beautifully modern and had a cozy fireplace. I drove from here to Nehalem with two other teachers.

At the end of my day it sometimes seemed a long long way. There were nights when the wind blew like fury as we drove along. The car was not new, and was a little on the ancient side. When the winds came in from the pounding ocean surf they came with such ferocity that I wondered sometimes if the car would suddenly be wrenched free and go bounding off. Then the three of us might be shaken and cast up somewhere perhaps along the way. In the late fall days when dusk fell so soon, we hurried to drive as fast as possible to get home. I had a wood burning range as well as the fireplace. It was a real hi-jinks to get home and get the fires going. Many evenings as the sun cast cold tongues of orange into the ocean as it dipped down, I brought the kitchen table into the living room so that I could have my supper in front of the fire.

Some nights the wind blew with hurricane force. (There was a storm door on both entrances to these duplexes which was a Godsend.) The wind blew so hard one night that it blew the hatch cover going to the attic off, and as I walked across the linoleum in the kitchen I was really treading on air.

One week-end the owners who lived in the other duplex went away on a vacation. It was a long-to-be-remembered week-end for me! I came home at the usual time and had put a steak on to fry. I had a good fire in the range, but was using the electric plate for the coffee. The wind began to kick up and I knew that it wouldn't be long before I would be in for a blow—a nasty one. I hurried with the meal.

When the steak was half done the lights suddenly went out, and I hustled around to get some candles lit. By that time I noticed that the fire in the range had gone out. I was just about to transfer the steak to the electric plate when I remembered—'no lights.'

At this juncture, the frigidaire had begun to defrost itself, obedient to the lack of power, and the drip was falling into a pudding I had made. Topping this I had discovered I was out of matches.

I put on a coat, tied up my head and inched down a stairway which led to the back yard. I was just going to cross the roadway to a neighbor for matches when I noticed there were some shingles flapping around the entrance to the apartment on the opposite side of mine.

I ran to see what was up.

The door to my manager's living room was swung wide open and was receiving the full force of the gale.

There wasn't a soul around!

I had an errie mixed feeling about this time. There was no family in the adjoining cottage on the other side. I couldn't understand how this door could have been left open. This was no time however for conjecture.

I now ran back again to the neighbor's. She had just managed to light her own candles. I said to her, "Just before the lights went out I thought I heard someone moving around there. It sounded to me as if they were tearing the place apart!"

Then I told her about the door being open and asked her if she would come up to my quarters to help me get my fire started. By this time my imagination had cleared the highest peak and before I had walked through the open door, I imagined the man and woman had quarrelled and he was taking the place apart!

The neighbor calmed me down, saying that there had been no one prowling, but there had been a man working there that afternoon, taking the storm door off and making a portico or housing to go over the entire doorway as a protection against the force of the wind, and that he probably hadn't closed the door too carefully on taking his leave, and the force of the wind had blown it open.

She went over with me and we closed things up first, then worked on my fire. After we had talked some few minutes, she went home.

After these many attempts, my fire was now burning brightly.

Just then SOMETHING blew around the corner of the house! It was the paper boy. He was all wet from head to foot; so also were all of his papers. I told him to stay and get warm and dry. We added more wood to the fire in the fireplace and we soon had that also blazing brightly. I put his socks up on the fire-screen to dry, made him a cup of cocoa and gave him part of my steak, which I had at last succeeded in cooking.

Looking out to sea, we could see the surf breaking over the 'Twin Rocks,' the tide was now going out, and the storm was subsiding at last. I called his mother and told her that he was all right and would be home soon. We had forgotten Buff, my kitten, who had begun to walk up and down in great contentment, enjoying the glowing fire!

10

Ne-Ah-Kah-Nie

Home Of The Great Fire Spirit

I had often spoken to my pupils about going on hikes and said that I would take some of them with me sometime. We spoke of Neahkahnie Mountain and the mysteries surrounding it. One of the teachers overheard me enthusing over the project, and they dismissed the issue with the remark that I would never climb THAT MOUNTAIN! And that I would give up long before I reached the top. Just then I made a mental reservation that 'we shall see!'

I had heard the legend of the Beeswax Ship and that there was a trail up the famed NE-AH-KAH-NIE Mountain. I decided one fine spring day that I would go to see for myself. Two of my pupils agreed to go with me as it was Saturday, and we had the day before us; we packed our own lunches.

We walked slowly out of Nehalem along the highway that approaches the mountain. We thought that if the opportunity presented itself we would hitch-hike a ride to the foot of the mountain. I wasn't too keen about taking a ride with strangers with my pupils, but thought that if we got tired enough we could perhaps ride part of the way in order to conserve our energies for the impending climb.

The very green new, fresh ferns made lacy patterns in the sun and shadows as we walked along; we noticed too the salmon berries growing along the way. Presently we arrived at the store at the crossroads going down into Manzanita. It was suggested that we take along some oranges and pop, as there would be no water on the mountain. I did not then realize how very greatly we would appreciate a means of quenching our thirst.

We had almost reached the meadow at the foot of the mountain when we got a ride with some friends to the beginning of the trail. There were no markers, those that had been there had been burned off with one of the many forest fires with which the area was ridden. We were then not too familiar with the starting point, but we slowly traversed the lower meadows as they rose gradually and gently.

The mountain grasses were burned and quite dry where the fire of the preceding summer had burned along one side of the mountain. We then covered foot by foot the places that had once known the games and laughter of Indian children in that far away time that the meadow had been known as Nika-Hyas-Se-Ah-Wust.

It was here that we ran into one of the stones that had been known and talked about for centuries. These Spanish stones left by the legendary crew who planted them as markers for the treasure that has been lost for so long. We looked the stone over carefully, trying to make out the hieroglyphics. There was a green lichen growing in these ancient impressions which we pushed out with sharp sticks. They were to us an enigma, but to the men who placed them there a sure pattern pointing the way to the treasure that has NEVER been found!

We were sure-footed at first, confident and fast moving. As the grade increased we found ourselves going slower and slower. We looked for the trail marked by the Conservation Corps in one of the preceding years but all marks had been totally obliterated.

Graceful wild flowers were beckoning fingers to us on the first part of the trail; we thought some of picking them but remembered the arduous climb ahead of us, and that we would be able to get all we wanted on the way down. We stopped to rest more and more frequently as we came to the greater heights. The sun had been climbing all the time with us and we realized when we reached the halfway mark why the mountain had been called: 'Home-Of-Fire-Spirit' by long ago tribes of Indians; we believed that it had perhaps not only been because of the inaccessibility and majesty of it. An appropriate title indeed! Our knees were beginning to have that parboiled you-won't-sleep-tonight-look.

Our progress became increasingly slower. We looked ahead, deciding which rock to tackle next. There were no trees at this point, just burned stubs that we couls grab occasionally. Still farther ahead we noticed a flat shelf or abutment of rock. We agreed that when we reached this point we would rest. Breathing heavily, we now attained the objective, and the glory of REST.

We sat in a row along this shelf of rock. We took off the scarves with which we had tied back our hair and tied the bottles of pop, one at each end, and slung them around our necks. One of the girls carried the rest of our lunch in a ruck-sack on her back. We made away with the oranges, each drank one extra bottle of pop but left the major part of the food for later.

Looking down now to the meadow, we saw a tiny red dot that appeared like a 'doodle bug' or small plane. It was a bulldozer that was breaking ground at the foot of the mountain. Only that morning the most recent hunt for the storied treasure had begun. (We later learned this was done by a partnership of Seattle-Portland capitalists.)

We were very tired now and I told the girls to rest and that I would sit and look. The girls immediately fell asleep. I looked down!

The mountain meadow, Manzanita, Nehalem, the long sand bar peninsula were now spread out flatly before me as an aerial map. Neahkahnie Lodge appeared as a miniature doll house at this elevation, and a toylike school which was ours; a smooth white cloud rode high above this picture.

I covered my eyes with my hands and in fancy beheld the crew of the storied Beeswax Ship making its way in single file toward the meadow from which we had come. In fancy I saw too a slight quivering of the bushes as the Indians were furtively watching them from their lacy hide-away. In this kaliedoscope of fancy many days passed before me. There was the toiling of the crew back over the rocks, dragging with chains the burdensome stones that would mark the treasure. Then! Behold! The final scene! Borne between several men was a heavy chest. A hole had been dug. They threw in the chest. The rock and soil was pushed back. They were finished! But wait, they were dragging before them a cowering creature. He was a black man. They killed him and threw his body where they had shoveled back some of the dirt. So! A black magic pervaded this scene. I saw on the shore a Spanish ship; it had listed to one side. Members of the crew were poling boatloads of gear ashore. The scene changes: it is now two days later. The galleon is not visible now except for her bow. The gear is reposing at different points along the beach. There are several dead bodies. Three large men are slowly coming to—as from a drugged sleep. They are rubbing their eyes and looking toward the mountain top, to Ne-Ah-Kah-Nie, home of the Fire Spirit and guardian of THEIR treasure!

* * *

I took my hands away and the present came flooding back in the haze of this mountain. Here are two sleeping girls, I must awake them, we must make the summit before dark!

We got gingerly to our feet, being somewhat stiff already. We had come now to the hardest part of our climb. The shalelike rock giving succor to our tired feet. The smaller of the two girls I left on a wide shelf or rock. She was too tired to go on and would wait for us.

The very top was now only about two hundred feet away. More crawling now, hand and hand. No sure footing on this slippery rock. A lost world found!—Now again this God given panorama—the mighty Pacific sweeping off into the haze!

A certain new dizziness now overcame us. For just a short while, leaning against a stone, we rested on a vicarious small flat place; we had reached the top, the highest point of land north of Mt. Tamalpais.

There was NO PATHWAY down either. We made our way at last to a lower level, finding again the shelf of rock that held our 'little lost sheep' who was by now wearing the dour troubled look that said, 'I want to go home.'

Yes, yes, we would go home. Our progress down the mountain was very fast. The girls got ahead of me in places. We came down in a little different direction from that in which we had come up. Most of the time here, there was no footing whatever. There were places where we had to turn around backwards to prevent the burned stubble from going into our eyes. Now we went along with our backs turned for some distance then facing down, slid along as on a huge toboggan slide. We landed at least half way down the mountain and sprawled into a cluster of protecting trees. Here in the soft grass we finished what was left of our lunch, throwing out the pop bottles just to hear and see them catapulting down to the bottom.

We came at last again to Nika-Hyas-Se-Ah-Wust, the meadow at the foot of the mountain. Now we picked all the beautiful mountain flowers that we wanted. This was our treasure trove; also to see the tiny wild babies, squirrels and rabbits that we surprised in their burrows as we progressed.

THE TRAIL'S END. We walked slowly along the highway praying some kind friend would happen by and pick us up. We felt like old mules, wearied and worn. We came again to the cross-roads store at the branching of the Manzanita road. Thirsty? Hungry? If we had been camels we could have accommodated no more liquid refreshment, this not being sufficient, we tapered off with hamburgers.

UP FORTH AGAIN! We clumped now down the highway toward Nehalem. Now, as we almost despaired, 'a sail on the starboard side,' rapid beckonings, smiles and greetings, a friend 'hove to'...........

I was dumped informally at my doorstep.

Back! Back again to the region of soft beds, and warm baths. The next day, and the next. Stiff? Yes, very, but happy.

Even though I hadn't left the five dollar bill up there under a rock as proof for the sceptical teacher who thought I would never made it. Hadn't I shaken hands with Ne-Ah-Kah-Nie, of storied legend and the Home of the Great Fire Spirit?

11
Nehalem Nostalgia

Memories! My children! My little fifth graders at Nehalem putting on their minstrel show! Ah, yes, we had the Mammly, Liza Jane and Suzanna, to say nothing of our reproduction of "The Camptown Races" with Hambone doing the gags in real grown-up style. Eddie Stanton and Joy Hansen doing their version of "Dark Town Strutters' Ball" (I'll be down to get you in a taxi, Honey).

At the noon hour when I had to black up twenty-two little faces in forty-five minutes, I reflected that if I could only have moved as fast as Walter Winchell talks, I could have been finished and back in a flash! Their childish wonder as each of their pals turned out with the mystery of a brand new black face. My little "Strutters" carrying off each bow to a 'T'.

At another time there was my turn when I took the part of Dahlia, the black maid, in a play given by the faculty. Me saying to Midnight, my colored spouse in the play, as I shifted a dollar bill to the top of my sock.

"Yere's one dollah you' ain' goin' be messin' 'roun' with!"

After our minstrel show, there were twenty-two little folks to be taken to the showers to be cleaned up after a good workout on their faces with cold cream. Then one of them saying to me, "Miz McNeil, mama says I can't black up again!" Then me remarking to them, "You know everybody does something like this once in a lifetime!"

The Finale, their bobbing heads swaying from side to side as they sang, "Shine On Harvest Moon" (I ain't had no lovin' since April, January, June or July) . . . .

These were slices of life that I would never forget!

12

Portland, My Tillicum

It was one A.M., the bellhop took me to the twelfth floor of the Benson Hotel, where there was one remaining accommodation. I was shown into a display room with its accompanying bedroom and bath.

I felt like a little lost chick. The room was so massive it was frightening. I listened as the footsteps of the attendant went echoing down the marble hallway toward the elevators.

I turned on all the flood lights to keep me company and until the newness of being there wore off.

My next thought was, 'Aha, my bill! My bill!" I phoned down and made inquiry. The desk clerk laughed and said, "Don't worry about that; you will be charged only the regular rate for the usual accommodation. I'm sure you will be able to sleep now."

Relief sung in my ears as I hung up. It was a snug world even if in the wee hours.

I went to the window and stuck my head out, looking up Broadway. The street lights were dancing a merry jig on the wet pavements.

I took off my gardenia and put it in a glass in the bottom of the tub. (It would be a good idea, as you couldn't get them for a song as you can in the South.)

And so to bed.

The following day, I was sitting in the ante room of Meier and Franks tenth floor tea room, waiting for a seat. I began to study the clothes of the people as they came in. I leaned over to the lady sitting next to me and said, "I like to watch the people as they come in, it gives one a chance to know what is being worn."

She looked me up and down with a quizzical I-wonder air and said, "Oh, are you a couturier?"

I didn't bat an eye but said in my most suave manner, "Oh, no, but it's interesting to note the various color combinations."

M-M-M. . . . All the rest of the day, I was filled with a sense of savoirfaire.

If Mother had been there she would have said that all the fun we used to have trying on hats in front of the mirror at home to kill a rainy afternoon was not lost.

(We learned that with a little finesse, one could put on any act, from the 'Flame of the Yukon' down. That was another stunt we did to make each other laugh; we started with 'The Lady That's Known As Lou' and did 'em all, down to 'Fresh Today,' the very vegetable woman who came to our back door every Tuesday.

Mama was a regular murderer of hats. She'd buy a perfectly good had with lots of style, bring it home and 'do something to it.'

Many times I came in unexpectedly at these moments, exclaiming while observing her latest sin: "Mama, how could you! And that WAS a nice hat, too!"

Amongest this conglomeration of 'Today's Women,' it was sad to note that there was an occasional murdered hat.

After I was finally settled at a table, I imagined that this was a special musical comedy, put on for my special benefit. I associated each person that came in with a song from some musical.

Among these there appeared "Mary." ("Mary, Mary—Mary is a grand old name, but for society and propriety they say Mah-rie"). Then came a versatile daisy with that 'You-were-meant-for-me' look! Now came a large blonde. She was electric, dressed in soft green, topped with a black shako. She was the epitome of Sophie Tucker, the "Some Of These Days" girl.

I played with my dessert as long as I could so I wouldn't miss anything.

An afternoon of shopping was dull after this!

I enjoyed the Oregon beach towns and their environs, but it was always pleasant to be able to glide away of a Friday afternoon, with my week's work behind me, for a week-end in Portland, or the joyous hour in flight that would bring me home to Seattle. And Portland! It was fun to find myself on a bus rolling unceremoniously under the Canyon Bridge, and dropping at last down into this city. Winking friendly lights seemed to reach out to me, inviting me into their very human encirclement.

From my room I could see at night the lighted homes on Council Crest, which gave me a cozy feeling of kinship.

Other nights from a different point, as I looked down Broadway I saw the varied colored lights of restaurants, theaters and other places of amusement. On rainy nights the brilliantly wet tops of cars which made their way on slick pavements, overlaid by the tooting of horns as each car asserted its impatience at the intersection.

I could always tell what time it was by the street noises. If I didn't go to sleep immediately, I heard as the night wore on the loud and devil-may-care laughter and talk of the late amusement clientele, over their echoing footsteps.

Later still, I heard the jarring and scraping sounds coming from the alley between the buildings.

I felt sorry for the garbage men because they had to break so many bottles as part of their work. Then there was the so familiar cat-soundtrack, cut off intermittently by the kaliedoscopic infusion of all other sounds.

I awoke to the early dawn twittering of the variety of birds having their sanctuary in the graceful rectangle of trees extending for about six blocks at the city's heart.

In the daytime as I strolled along through this area, I thought that the donors must have been far seeing when they envisioned the informality and restfulness that would one day emanate from this magical square.

I heard the Journal clock, illuminated at night, ring out the hours in booming 'Big Ben' style, to tell me that this city was not a dream but a reality!

It was no dream, all this was real, and Portland, city of Roses, was my Tillicum!

13
Unknown Village

I came slowly down the wide, windswept street of Westport Washington, bordered on one side by small store buildings. I had not planned on cooking my meals, and so at this early hour before the opening of the first day of school, I was looking for a place where I could have my breakfast.

I came down to the far end of the street to the place where the road turns to go toward the beach. There was a large store building there. There was a fountain where they served hamburgers, where I thought I might be able to get at least a cup of coffee. I eased myself up on one of the stools. There was a man conversing in loud tones on the other side. Some people who appeared to be tradesmen were coming and going. I waited. Nothing happened. No one paid the least attention to me.

I felt heartsick as I had not known that it would be so hard just to get a bit of breakfast. There was nothing doing. I knew that I was wasting my time sitting there so I went out again, walking slowly down the length of the street. When I had reached the opposite end, I went into the store there where I made further inquiry only to find that there was no place at all serving meals. As I turned to go out, the storekeeper called to me and said, "If you don't mind being informal, you can have a cup of coffee with us."

I joined this friendly family group in their quarters in back of the store. After all that walking and wishing, this came as a welcome break. I didn't like to infringe on their privacy but there was no alternative.

The first month of school I stayed at an apartment court, the accommodations of which were all very fine, but the outlay for rent was too much for the salary I was making. At the end of that time I was successful in engaging a 'room.' It was very pleasant and I liked it because it was situated on the third floor at the top of the house more or less by itself. I thought this would be a good place for anyone like me who wanted to read and do some writing during my spare time.

The window of this room looked out towards the harbor. Here I could see occasional boats enroute to Aberdeen. There were, too, three large fir trees swinging in the wind. This was an adequate and pleasant place during the early fall.

During the close of the month of November, a terrific storm blew up. The house quivered and shook and I thought that at any moment it might be taken off its foundations. At the height of the storm, water began coming in around the windows, making a slow trickle across the floor. The following week I moved to the floor below where it was warmer and more sheltered from the wind. It was cozy enough, but I missed my sanctuary near the tops of the giant firs. There was a constant noise from the comings and goings of other tenants and the banging of the front door. Also a loud hum of voices always came up through a hot air register in the floor.

I could forget these things later in the evening, however, when upon getting ready for bed I pushed my bed close to the open window where I could breathe in the pure air on a still night and watch the movement of the trees across the sky. The beams from the lighthouse flashed intermittently through the branches and I watched, too, the headlights of the cars as they made their way across the Elk River bridge. Stargazing then and much time for reflection before falling off to sleep.

This was an economical way to live but had its drawbacks. The 'room' had no equipment for the preparation of a meal. I bought a small coffee maker on which I prepared all my meals. The only time I really was stymied was when I tried to fry a small piece of steak on it. It simply wasn't hot enough but after lining for many months out of cans, even an underdone steak had its possibilities.

Then there were the Fridays, DEAR FRIDAYS. Having no car of my own, I usually hitch-hiked into Aberdeen, as busses to Westport only operated about three times a week, except for one bus into the city which did not arrive until seven P.M. It was fun, after being inside all week to buzz out, my little carry-all in my hand, and get the fresh invigorating air in my lungs. What if it did rain, and the wind blow? I honestly enjoyed the wind and air anyway.

The people down on this peninsula were the world's best friends when it came to giving me a lift. During the three years that I spent here, I had a lift from just about everyone, light man, telephone man, fisherman, sportsmen, and even the milkman.

One of these times, however, my lift was going only as far as the 'Y' or branching of the road. It was a beautiful spring day and I sauntered slowly along, presently approaching a level strip of highway on one side of which there was low lying brush. Paralleling the highway on the other side was a wide ditch filled with water.

As I walked along, my nose in the air enjoying the fresh greenery and freedom, I began to hear slight rustlings in the brush. I looked around, but saw nothing, so continued my walk. More time passed. Now I began to notice that a whole herd of cows was following me on the other side of the ditch. There were papa cows, mama cows, baby cows, both 'bullets' and heifers. They were all bauling and clanking as they came. I wondered, WHAT HAVE I DONE TO DESERVE THIS? I saw that they all had white faces similar to those seen on the ranges of Montana.

The bulls of the outfit seemed to be taking quite a fancy to me. They walked along as close to me as they could get. Just as I began to think and to hope that they wouldn't jump the ditch, a car slowed down and I had a lift to Aberdeen!

I felt rather silly but couldn't keep from smiling. The driver must have wondered 'What goes?' and thought that I was perhaps a little weak in the head. Nice cows, nice walk, nice scenery, but man alive! I had heard the cows and herded them, walked with them and now this wonderful lift.

There were Fridays when I would have walked for a considerable distance before being picked up. The general reaction of the attendant at the Morck Hotel was "I wonder what she is up to now?"

One time I came in after two lifts, I noticed a rather tall blond man established at a desk in the corner of the lobby. (I thought for a moment that I was seeing Sydney Greenstreet in a movie.) This time playing the role of 'Travel Agent.' He was really Eric Ekmark of a local travel bureau.

I loved the trees, breeze and the wafted perfume of the dear Pacific, but it was another kind of delight to come into town and rub elbows with the crowd. I sailed down Wishkah Street at about the same time many week-ends. The people were very friendly. They got so they wondered how she got in this Friday. I always felt breezy and happy at these times. It gave me a pleasant feeling inside as having people interested in you is all that counts.

When I got up in my room I took off my 'Sloppy Joes,' changed my clothes and tidied my hair; I felt as much changed as a chameleon as I rode down again in the elevator. On the way down, I put on a 'Vogue' air as I screwed the last earring into place and put on my I-love-everybody happy face.

I usually made the outgoing bus connection from Aberdeen to return to Westport, but one night I missed the bus and wondered how I would get to school the next morning. That night I inquired at the dairy the time of departure of the milk truck and arranged to be picked up at Wolff's Corner about six-forty-five A.M.

I seemed to stand there a long time; numerous trucks went by with the Smith label, and I thought a great how-de-do if he misses me. When I had begun to despair of being picked up at all, the truck pulled up to the curb. I climbed in on the starboard side. The buss was loaded to the absolute limit, four canvas rolls containing the ice cream were strapped to the running boards.

Our progress was very slow, as we made all the little stops along the way, but our speed was increased after we crossed the Elk River bridge. I got off at the main intersection of the highway, and walked the rest of the way over to school.

The children were all lined up and sitting along the fence. The bell had not yet rung and there were only about three minutes left. The milkman had saved the day.

During the first few weeks I was at Westport, I was more or less on the *qui vive?* for possible places to eat, and walks that would be any slight change from routine.

One foggy Saturday I was on my way down to Westhaven, the place that later was to become the great Westport fishing area. I was sprinting along, my head in the air, and listening to the oft repeated blasts of the fog horn. The wind was blowing rather coldly and my hair was doing a witch's dance across my face. My spirits were somewhere 'in the bottom of the bucket'!

As I came to the part of the road where there were no houses, a long lonely waste of road, deserted at this late afternoon hour, I was thinking too that perhaps I looked a little odd trailing down there all by myself, I heard someone calling, "Yoo-hoo, yoo, hoo, where are you going?" A woman's head was protruding from the upstairs window of a house on the overhanging cliff.

I pointed down towards the docks, saying, "Going down to Westhaven for dinner," then she replied, "How about a cup of coffee?"

Then I replied, "No, but thanks a lot." I felt that I had made myself too conspicuous and I was too independent to take gratuity from someone that I didn't know. Almost immediately after that a car came along, taking me the rest of the way.

I found a small restaurant where I had a good dinner, and everything tasted grand after my long walk. By the time I had finished it was quite dark. At that time there was a taxi operating from the anchorage area, so I got home without getting any more sand in my shoes.

14

Maria and Mabel

I would never have known Maria if I had done no hitchhiking. She picked me up one Friday afternoon. We found that we were interested in the same things, music and books. She was a congenial hail-fellow-well-met type, the kind of person to be admired by man. I had spent some very lonely days when I was not with my children and it was a pleasure to meet someone like this. She was my star who brought me luck.

She came to see me soon after our first meeting, and that same afternoon she asked me to dinner. We had an interesting musical time of it. She was a natural when it came to the piano and could play any type of music in any tempo. During the evening, some little children living next door to her came in. Maria was a kindred loving spirit to them. They all gathered around the piano as she played.

She took one of the smaller tots on her lap, playing and telling them little stories as she went along. The children watched her with loving and intrigued eyes. All this time I was thinking what good fortune to know such a person. God had been good to me to bring us together.

After the tots left, there was laughing and much hilarity. We even talked some of hiring a hall and giving a two piano concert. Very little inducement would have been needed for me, especially after I had heard her rendition of George Gershwin's "Rhapsody in Blue."

She wrote to me during the summer, telling me she had put up some wild-blackberry jam. We would be sharing again in the fall the music and companionship of each other. She had said in a letter:

"We'll let the wild waves roar, and the fog horn blow its loudest on winter evenings."

Life was good when it held people like Maria!

Mabel was another with heart of gold. She was tall, slender, dark-eyed and walked with an easy grace. She often came in for an evening and told me interesting stories of her young childhood. She told me of a quaint old-fashioned soul, and old lady who wore a capacious apron and small cap and always carried peppermints in her pocket. These she gave to Mabel for going on errands for her. Mabel still treasures the cap which belonged to this personality lovingly referred to as 'Aunt Net.'

Mabel lived in a little house in the woods adjacent to both the school and where I lived. I often visited her there. She could cook steaks as a master chef. She, her husband Paul and I had dinner to the accompaniment of much friendly banter as we reviewed events of the day, or anything of moment that had gathered some sparks.

Here I could hear the trees swaying in the night wind; looking out one could see the giant tree branches as they swung in the arc of the recurring flashes from the lighthouse.

There was more than a 'latch-string' out in this little house, there was a feeling of sharing; an open-hearted friendliness that is not found on every doorstep!

15

Clouds Flying

My very first flight was a flight between Seattle and Spokane in 1947. It occurred in the days when you never could be sure of a seat and might be 'bumped' after being all packed up and waiting down at Boeing Field with an expectant face.

I was 'bumped' before I ever got off the ground, all checked in, baggage weighed and everything. I was looking wonderingly out on the field, expecting my trip number to be called at any time.

Now the loudspeaker was paging myself and another lady. We moved simultaneously deskward.

She was beautifully dressed, be-diamond, be-flowered and well coifed.

And there was ME, oh, just there was me! (Friends would have said that was enough.)

We were both informed in a very polite tone that our seats had been taken for military personnel (War time, you know).

Suddenly this beautiful woman burst out crying loudly so all present could hear, "Oh, I'll miss my connections, I'll miss my connections!"

Must have been SOME connections!

I decided to sit it out and wait for the first cancellation.

Mentally skylin-ing the people as I sat there proved to be great sport. Over in one corner was a small company of soldiers wearing overseas coats with fur lined caps, sitting on their duffle bags (probably Aleutian bound). A handsome, light-colored couple came in and as they approached there was that perfume smell.

A plane had just arrived from Hawaii. Among the people who got off was a whole family dressed in tropical apparel. They were wearing fresh leis, which went well with their tanned legs. Papa, however, had on light plus-fours.

My turn at last! This after a two hour wait. I suppose most people would have given up in despair, but not THIS gal. I had little shivers inside after the departure was announced and I was walking out on the field for the first time.

I almost stubbed my toe and fell down climbing the ramp, I was so excited.

By the time I got on, all the seats were taken except in the rear, so I took the last seat (the tail seat). The stewardess, wishing to encourage me, said, "Oh, you'll like the tail seat!"

Excited? Oh no? I felt something like you do when you know you are going to take gas for the first time.

The plane slowly taxied down the field. I thought: Isn't it a shame to die when you've got so many more things to do! The pilot revved up the motors. I thought: Oh, I knew it wouldn't work!

As we spun off the ground, I said a little prayer to my patron saint, all the time hanging onto the seat arms with a death grip.

THEN . . . I was in a boat sailing off into 'the high blue yonder!'

What a ninny I had been to be so frightened! The only thing I didn't like was that the curtains had to be buttoned over the windows until we were well off the field (War time).

Presently they were unbuttoned. What mystery to look down on the highways with their accountrement of bugs of all colors speeding on their various ways. Far little miniatures.

I reflected what a privilege to be able to fly. I had always envied 'The Little Lame Prince' his magic cloak. Ever since in childhood I had read the story I had thought: wouldn't it be nice to be able to get away from it all in such a fascinating manner!

Here was I—no lame princeling—but able to walk and fly as well. God was good to me because He gave me this chance.

We were flying now toward the Pass (Blewett). The sun was gently tinging the mountain peaks. From the top of Mt. Ranier rosy rays dispersed themselves into the circle of gathered clouds that seemed to bubble forth from the top like an over-burdened tub of suds.

What a wonder this skyland rim!

The stewardess was the kind that gave you a warm feeling inside. Rolling gently along, flying at higher altitude than the strata of clouds holding cross winds and cord-like bumps. We were served breakfast aloft; orange juice, a butterhorn and coffee, this being only a short flight.

A large fat man sat in front of me. He puffed and puffed every time he had to fasten and unfasten his seat belt. Over the slight vibrational waves, it was possible to hear the friendly chatter of the nearer passengers. They were talking with the stewardess who spoke to all, giving out and information of general nature requested.

Now we were over Eastern Washington, the sun merging with the squared off plats of the wheat fields. We passed occasional silos, railroads and small towns.

We did not fly over the Grand Coulee Dam as it was taboo in wartime. And so, down on the field at Spokane. What a 'let down' to have to come down to earth!

Did I like flying? As the 'cullud' would have said,

"Chile, ah ain't goin' mess wid de groun' no mo', yu onerstan' dat? Ah is takin' wings, ah is!"

The winter of '46-'47, I was the only teacher commuting regularly on most week-ends by air between Grays Harbor and Seattle. Interspersed between these Aberdeen-Seattle trips were monthly trips to Portland. I rode 'em rough, and I rode 'em smooth.

I rode on the fourth commercial flight off Moon Island. I would have flown on the initial flight, but it took place on a school day.

Fun? All I cared about during off hours were these trips. No two were alike.

I began to know the topography of the route rather well between these points. The brisk takeoff into the wind, sailing then on smooth days, gently over the West Seattle hill, over Bow Lake, Three Tree Point, Vashon Island, Maury Island, McNeil Island, and thence over Nisqually Reach and the maze of small land formations and other waterways, down the sound to Olympia.

Our State Capitol made its own place in our hearts as well as on the living map before us. On a cloudy day it seemed as if a fairy hand always shoved the clouds away and let a brief sun shine on the Capitol dome, just to let one know that this city was set apart, Olympia, our Capitol City!

Down at Olympia and swerving off, buzzing McCleary, Elma, Montesano, then following the valley down.

Coming rather abruptly around the little 'Gibraltar' hiding Aberdeen there is a cozy sign on this bluff reading: "Pioneer." Yes, I thought, how appropriate! The West Coast Air Lines pioneer air route to Grays Harbor!

The pilots and co-pilots were democratic and friendly, and I began to know them all. I had asked for some of the technical data regarding these ships, and I received the following letter from David R. Bath, West Coast pilot.

76 SAND IN MY SHOES

West Coast Airlines
Georgetown Station
Seattle, Washington
June 13, 1947

Dear Mrs. McNeil,

It is a pleasure to hear from you, and feel your interest and enthusiasm for our airline. We are always happy to have you aboard in your usual seat, last seat aft, starboard side.

In the following paragraphs I will attempt to put down some information concerning our operation, though I warn you, it will be colored by a "Throttle Bender's" perspective.

West Coast operates the D.C. twin engine, twenty-four passenger Douglas transport. The ship is powered with two 1250 horsepower Engines, either of which is capable of taking the ship off and negotiating a safe landing with the other engine inoperative. The aircraft with the load weighs over twelve tons. Four fuel tanks carry eight hundred gallons of gasoline which is consumed by the hungry engines at the rate of one hundred gallons per hour. The ship cruises at an average speed of 170 miles an hour . . .

. . . The aircraft is operated by a crew of three; pilot, co-pilot and flight attendant. It requires the use of two men on the flight deck. The pilot seated on the left side does the flying while the co-pilot on the right watches the engine temperatures and pressures, operates various mechanisms at the pilot's command and handles all radio contacts.

Pilot training is an important consideration to any airline. West Coast continually stresses its two main objectives to the pilots—safety and passenger comfort. Our pilots average thirty-one years of age and have accumulated four thousand three hundred hours of flying. They all have been flight checked by the Civil Aeronautics Authority, and have been granted an Airline Pilot Certificate. This insures the traveling public that pilot personnel are safe and competent.

The company has subjected each pilot to a rigid flight training program, to enable him to handle the aircraft under any conditions it might encounter. Considerable time is spent practicing blind flying and operating the ship on one engine.

Every six months of a pilot's career, he is subjected to a grueling flight check, at which time he must re-prove his efficiency. Failure to come up to standards results in going back to co-pilot.

. . . Piloting is a profession that never grows dull. The

boundless parorama of nature always unfolding before your eyes is a continual source of inspiration. You come to know and love each tree, boulder, highway and cottage. Nature yields many of her secrets to airborne eyes—the patterns of drainage ribbons, the meandering of streams, the selection of certain tree species to a particular environment, rock faults and glacial effects on a grand scale. (And it's a perfect way to select a secluded fishing haunt.) Working in Mother Nature's weather factory is fun. Watching the approach of a storm with its accompanying cloud warnings and knowing how to navigate safely through gives a feeling of accomplishment.

As for the lighter side of the airline business, there are many incidents occurring daily which bring on the smiles.

On the occasion of a rather hard landing that jarred the uppers of the passengers, after the ship had rolled to a stop, the flight attendant came forward to the flight deck bearing a business card of a bulldozing contractor. On the reverse side was written the offering that he would be glad to bring his bulldozer out and scrape off that big bump at the end of the runway!

All new flight attendants on their first flight are usually indoctrinated by the flight crew by a special ruse. A flight on which there are no passengers is selected. As the flight attendant reads or dozes back in the cabin, the co-pilot and the pilot set the controls on the automatic pilot, scotch tape a pair of gloves to the control wheel and then both seats are abandoned for the baggage pit just aft the seats, but hidden. The buzzer is then sounded, summoning the flight attendant forward . . . The unsuspecting lad saunters forward to the flight deck and sees only a pair of gloves guiding the great iron bird. With hair raised and wild eyed, he charges back into the cabin!

If you are able to reclaim any ideas from the above conglomeration, please use them as you see fit!

Sincerely,
(signed) David R. Bath.

I rode with Pilot Russel Bath at the controls many times. There was always something new, as flight, any flight, presents many changing aspects. It was smooth most trips. We glided over the ocean sometimes, but when the winds were bad we flew inland.

I recall one particular day. We were off Moon Island Airport about five minutes. The sun was shining, a brief break in the cloud formation showed a pretty little village clearly outlined with its doll-like roofs and fringes of trees. I saw the long sandy peninsula with its toy light house, and without thinking I inquired, "What is the name of that pretty little village?"

He answered, "That? Why that is Westport!"

Right about then I was recalling the many times I had hiked along this road, the wind blowing fiercely in my ears, never being sure of my lift and I thought: Ah ha! The hiking was worth it if I could buck-board the clouds!

I was due out of Portland that following Sunday afternoon. There was a stiff breeze blowing and the sky looked threatening. There had been a delay of about an hour and a half before the West Coast came in, due to the unsettled weather. I had been sitting in the waiting room. I couldn't help but hear the general talk between the attendants as the teletype was coming through. The possibilities of getting off for Grays Harbor looked pretty slim. Several people came in and there wasn't much encouragement given.

Then a man came in. He was a first flighter. The attendants told him he should cancel his trip if he felt at all squeamish about it. This he did.

They decided to take off with the mail about four o'clock. I was the only passenger, and riding tail seat. It really was a growler. The attendant asked me if I wouldn't care to ride farther forward, as it perhaps wouldn't be so bumpy.

I countered with, "No, thanks, I like the bumps and I'll help hold the tail down for you."

We bounced and bounced. A heavy downpour of rain, a dull drab looking sky. The chains on the doorway clanked around like a knight in full armor walking the graveyard shift. (These were covered with rubber subsequently.) We flew steadily, if bumpily, along the river, then inland.

We went down at Astoria just long enough to drop the mail sacks. There had been some talk of not going down at Moon Island, and grounding at Olympia on account of the storm. The attendant asked, "How is it?" as he threw off the mail.

The answer was "Just like silk!"

They found that "hole" in the muggy cloud wall and we went down at Moon Island. The landing lights looked pretty good to me. It was just getting dark (no radio beam at that time). Crossing the field, there was about four inches of water. I was wet but I certainly had a ride and found out about 'those bumps.' The general runs to Portland were rather uneventful. It was interesting to see the faces the earth turned up with weather. Some of the time we flew inland, flying over Bear Creek Ridge, Green Mountain, Mt. Nickoli, Wickiup,

Saddle and Humbug. All these lesser peaks with a shining Mt. St. Helens often visible in the distance.

One trip in we circled low on the approach to the Portland Field. A small plane was on the strip. I looked up and the gentle slope of hilltop homes seemed to be spinning around overhead . . . With the sky somehow mixed up under my feet. The plane seemed a lot bigger then as it spun around slowly, killing time for a landing.

Returning to Grays Harbor one week-end, we flew low along Long Beach. It was the occasion of the Annual Clam Bake. Here and there I could see the cars buzzing along the beach; parents hustling around over the food problem; some were playing baseball on the beach, others were wading and swimming.

Leaving the beach at Leadbetter Point, we crossed an area of small coves with some rocky promontories. In the bright sun everything stood out in clear relief, the green stalwart trees with the sleeping inshore waves lapping the coves and other irregular areas.

I saw several wrecks with their decks awash. The most recent one a lumber boat that had been beached in a storm. It was painted navy gray, and except for the decided list and the realization that she was stuck in the sand, I could imagine it a toy boat that had been cast there by the hand of a happy child.

Leaving the Point, I could see the waves breaking on the beach like wisps of meringue on a pie.

One Saturday morning, leaving Moon Island for Seattle, we took on a bride and groom. The whole wedding party had come down to bid them Bon Voyage. There was considerable laughing, hoking, picture taking and rice throwing. The plane was delayed a moment or two while last goodbyes were being said.

It was fun watching them try to rid themselves of their cargo of telltale rice. During the trip, the pilot came down to congratulate them, and pass out stogies.

16
Westport Coast Guard

Sand, sand, sand. I was going down to the Coast Guard Station at Westport. Mr. W. G. Kincaide, Chief Bosun's Mate, officer-in-charge, took me down there; I wanted to get some information about it. It was a windswept place. Sand dunes bubbling off to the line of surf breaking on the beach. It was the same one I had gone down that lonely afternoon in search of a meal.

Now it was early spring. Much water had gone through the scuppers since my first visit to this stretch of sand. It seems Mr. Kincaide and I each had our individual problems, as he remarked to me one day when he came to visit school during the noon hour. My back was turned to the doorway and I didn't see him come in—I was leading the rhythm band, pounding out "The Man On The Flying Trapeze" —I heard a voice say, "You couldn't use a tenor, could you?" Tsk, tsk. We went in the station the back way, handiest to the road. As we entered, I noted a small black puppy.

I said, "Oh, he's eating a hotcake," and Mr. Kincaide replied, "Oh no, not a hotcake, a pork chop." I thought: what a lucky pup to have a pork chop all to himself. I think, however, as the new mascot he was an important link in the chain that guards our coastline—and thus entitled to the best there is.

The station had three decks. There were offices and recreation rooms on the first floor, together with officers quarters. The second deck was given over to barrack room sleeping quarters for the enlisted personnel. There was an attic then being used for storage purposes. A loft was in the bell tower. The watches were kept by the use of an ordinary watchman's clock. It had a paper dial which automatically punched the record, of arriving and leaving.

In the period of the recent war, the enlisted personnel was augmented to sixty. At the period of writing there were only fifteen. It was said at that time twenty would be the best number.

In the basement there was another recreation room with a ping pong table. In front of the station was a rain guage with an inking device. This was read and changed twice weekly.

Mr. Kincaide gave me the following information:

Up to October 1946, there were three Coast Guard units at Westport. The Lifeboat Station with fifteen enlisted men and one officer, the Radio Station with twenty-three enlisted men and one officer, and the Light Station with three enlisted men.

In October the Light Station was operationally divided, wherein the Radio Station was charged with the operation of the Light and Lifeboat Stations, making them responsible for the operation of the radio beacon and the fog signal.

Radio Westport is the principal communications station of the "Thirteenth Coast Guard District," handling all radio traffic of Marine interest in the Northwest. They received reports from all ships both commercial and federal, and transmitted many messages each day, including weather reports and notices to mariners. A continuous twenty-four hour watch is maintained on six frequencies.

A new fifty thousand dollar radio station was recently placed in operation (in the '50's). It was located at Westport, not for geographical reasons, but the Westport location was found by experiments to be the best for radio reception and transmission in the entire Northwest.

The Lighthouse, important from a mariners' standpoint, is actually simple in operation. It is electric and to turn it on or off involves the mere flicking of a switch. Grays Harbor Lifeboat Station is the busiest of all Lifeboat Stations in the Thirteenth Coast Guard District and answers more calls for assistance than any other station on the Coast. All Lifeboat Stations have a variety of calls for assistance; Grays Harbor is unique only in having a wider variety.

After showing me the station proper, Mr. Kinkaide took me out on a catwalk pier. This led to the boathouse. There I saw a pulling surf boat, length twenty-six feen and a twenty-six foot power boat. The power boat is self-bailing, all the water coming out through the scuppers.

Others there were a thirty-six foot motor life boat, finished in teak inside; the outside being oak; a thirty-eight foot picket boat which is used in trailing and overtaking. It was to be painted white with varnished rail. The boat of greatest interest allotted to the Westport Station was the Lifeboat "Invincible." It is fifty-two feet in length.

Of these boats there are only two in America, the other "The Triumph" was despatched to the Point Adams Station.

Before these boats were built, the federal government sent to England as well as to some of the Scandinavian countries for boats of this unusual kind.

Mr. Kincaide has had several young boys giving their initial service here. He took a brotherly interest in them. He told me some of the boys needed encouragement and bolstering at times. I was told of one lad who had wept with loneliness; he had made a wrong representation of his age.

Harold Olaf Hansen was mentioned as having a 'lot of what it takes.' He had just nine months left to complete his course when he was called to the service. He completed his course by home study while dispatching his duties. He went home graduating with his class, on fifteen days leave.

As we came out again, the tide was higher, a dull fog was fast settling and I could hear the booming of the fog horn. This eerie, ever-present sound is a just reminder of the Coast vigil. With all the mechanisms proper to this modern station, there will always be an aura of romance, not entirely built on the history of the coastline in the past. The privilege of my visit to Westport Coast Guard Station will always be a treasured memory.

17
A Beacon Seaward

The Phantom Fleet

On the long midwatch, when the moon is dim,
And the clouds go scudding by,
When the old ship rolls with the heaving swell,
And the spume comes flying high;
A tale is told of a Phantom Fleet,
Which came like the silent dawn.
With never a creak of block or line
And yet, goes sailing on.

They are the ghosts of the sailing ships
That sank on the roaring main,
That rise at night from Neptune's realm
To battle the storm again.
For many a lone windjammer's crew
Have died on the stormy deep,
Where only the seagulls know their graves,
And only the mermaids weep.

The seaweed hangs from their sagging rails,
The barnacles gleam like stars,
But the old romance of the clipper ships
Still clings to their broken spars.
Their phantom crews are up on deck,
With salt crust in their hair,
And their eyes are fixed on the leaping waves,
With a bold, defiant stare.

> Thus on nights when the Storm King rules,
> And the sea is a foaming spray,
> The Phantom Fleet like a mist appears,
> Then fades like a dream away.
> —Lt. (j.g.) Harry E. Helgeson
> Astoria, Oregon

With the sun slowly dunking itself in the ocean, I stopped at North Cove. Here a number of years ago the lighthouse had slipped gradually into the sea. There was little left to remind one of this catastrophe. Quoting from the *Aberdeen World*, of December 25, 1940: "The North Cove Lighthouse has been caught in the bight of the eternal battle between shore and sea. Today the surf lapped at the very bricks of the main foundation and had undermined a small projecting portion of the building, leaving it hanging in mid-air. In a few, perhaps one, surely in a week or two, the ocean will churn the supporting sand away and the old light will topple. When it does an eventful career is ended."

The lighthouse had been built on Cape Shoalwater, the sea and harbor currents gradually have worn the sands of the cape away so there is no cape there anymore.

I looked out toward the darkening sea. I could see again the many events that this landmark had been a setting for in the parade of the years. The ancient wrecks had bent clammy beckoning fingers for the guarding tower to join them into their flight to eternity. I could not roam over this area without wanting to know the events of the years beyond average memory that had held so much of hope, fear and despair in days long gone.

I sat back on a log. I closed my eyes and dreamed of these events, the long parade of them fading from everyday memory, some of them like the old wrecks sinking gradually into the sand.

Frank Peterson of Westport was a youngster in swaddling clothes when the foundation of the light was laid in 1858 and had a close attachment for the light. Its beams were welcoming when Peterson used to drive his freight and mail-lugging team along the beach. The station often sheltered him.

In 1940 Mr. Peterson went up into the tower for the first time in fifty-five years. He found it then much the same, even to the nick in the prism lens made by a coot, which in the time of Keeper Stream sailed down "before the wind," crashed through the plate glass window and practically "splashed" all over the light.

Peterson recalled at the time the very first turning on of the light. It was fed with lard oil.

Then the keepers used to climb the stairs with a feather soaked in turpentine to prime the wick so that it would take fire easily.

One of the strange regulations was that no matches were permitted in the lens room atop the tower, but a keeper was permitted to carry a lighted torch from below to light the wick. Then the clockwork rotating the lens was wound every two hours.

There is the story of Christian K. Zauner, who had been famous and faithful keeper of the North Cove Light.

After twenty-seven years he had retired. In the early days of his stay, Wesport had been a bustling town, and was considered to have an equal chance with rival towns up the river in the race for population.

Mr. Zauner had told of the turning on of the big light for the first time, and how in that early day it had sent its beams faithfully out, giving warning over bay and ocean. Great ship traffic in those days consisted of two or three small steam schooners or two sailing vessels entering and leaving the harbor each week.

Numerous fishing boats used the port, but it was never thought that ten thousand ton ships would one day be sailing over the treacherous Grays Harbor bar.

The first light was furnished by an oil lamp containing four huge wicks. These wicks later were replaced by incandescent mantles which were also lighted by oil. The powerful lenses had to be carefully polished every day. The oil was drawn up ninety feet, strained and filtered. The one fourth inch glass surrounding the lantern room had to be washed and polished and the long winding stairs had to be kept spotlessly clean.

Three keepers worked in alternate shifts, one going on at sunset, and working to midnight, the second working from midnight to sunrise. Each man had one night off in three, but on bad nights when the fog horn had to be operated, the entire force frequently worked all of the time.

This light on a fairly clear night was visible to all within an eighteen mile radius. The lantern room was reached by one hundred forty-seven steps that spiraled their way upward in eight flights around the tower. The motive power for the light was furnished by machinery that resembled a giant clock, a two hundred pound pendulum was wound up every day. It slowly moved downward each eight hours.

This pendulum, too, was an indicator of earthquakes. It recorded the earthquake at San Francisco in 1906.

The famous North Cove Light saw many sights. So many men

have struggled for their lives within scope of this light that even Uncle Sam has lost count. In the ancient musty records are tales of heroism, death, and joyous rescue. The havoc of storms, the happy arrival and departure of all manner of ships, most of them long forgotten.

The "Abbie Cooper" crashed ashore virtually under the rim of the lighthouse in 1884. Then only a few months later, on January 18, 1885, the "Dewa Gungadhar," an English squarerigger, came drifting in stern first, comint to rest athwart the "Abbie Cooper," which had settled in the sand.

The procession of wrecks in the eighties included the "Great Broughton," "Grace Roberts," and the "Whistler"; followed in the nineties by the "Glenmorag" and "Strathblane." At the turn of the century, there was the "Potlatch," a big British four-mast bark which went ashore in 1901 and by good fortune remained intact. It was rolled overland to a safe launching later. In 1905, the "C.A. Klose"; 1907, the schooner "Solano," a large steamer; the Canadian "Caoba" in 1925. There were other ships doubtless whose bones still rest somewhere in the sands, of which all memory is erased.

When the North Cove light was built the beach was more than a mile away and the builders confidently believed the light would stand for centuries. But they did not reckon with the shifty currents that pour out of the long southern arm of Willapa Bay and westward from Willapa River. Deepwater ships now plow inbound and outbound over the very spot where oldtimers dug clams!

I first dreamed of these events then I read of them. Now I was looking slowly out to the darkening sea. I could see the waves breaking over the bar. They looked higher than the shore line and broke somewhere betwixt the farthest horizon and the skyline. The brisk cooling breezes were playing havoc with my hair as I sat there on this lonely stretch of beach. I imagined the storm winds breaking over the bar, lifting ships like popping corks and smashing them to their doom.

IT WAS NO DREAM.

This lighthouse had held in the palm of her hand the whole parade. Then weakening her grasp she too had met her fate.

18

Peninsula Pete

One Saturday morning I went down to Westhaven for a walk. I had just reached the top of the ramp leading to the barge restaurant when I heard a commotion on the dock. There was Peninsula Pete sloshing his way down, at none too steady a gait.

He was 'looking at the world through rose colored glasses.' He came in just after I did, and ordered himself a side of ham and some eggs.

I noticed Jason was there, too, holding forth in his very best. He was saying: "Hey! Pete, goin' home tomorrah?" One of the others chimed in with, "M-m-m—The way you've been goin' lately, the doc'll sure have to look you over."

Down at the far side of the counter I could see Oscar who I understood was dependable, and knew when to keep his mouth shut, but this time I could see that the temptation was too great.

"Hey Pete, what about that girl you were telling me about?"

Pete didn't say very much, he just went on eating. I could see by his face, though, that he was doing a lot of thinking. He was annoyed, but in the rosy haze that enveloped him, I suppose he found it too much exertion to have a comeback.

Then the door opened again and Walt came in. A long glower passed between them. The rest of the men at the counter began to slow down. I guess they could see that their remarks weren't going over with Pete. They concluded that it wouldn't do much good to make him real sore.

I saw Walt come slowly down the length of the room. He settled himself on the stool next to Pete. They both were still glowering at each other. Nothing was said. The steaks went right on frying themselves.

Now Walt leaned over toward Pete, and I heard him say in a confidential but meaningful tone, "I hear you're goin' home." Pete fastened on Walt a pie-eyed but baleful look and said, "And whose business is it if I don't? You wanted that extra cut on the fish, didn't you?"

I could see Walt giving him a quizzical look. He acted as if he just couldn't make up his mind. I knew that Walt thought a lot of the girl.

I was sorry for Walt, because Pete was known only to be faithful to the "Star Dust." He never had let HER down. He always came down in a big blow to watch the lines. Pete had told me that he had put in twelve or fourteen hours watching the "Star Dust," and waiting for the wind to change, then he would go home and catch a little sleep.

The rest of their conversation was muffled and I couldn't hear any more. As I walked down the ramp again to the dock, a brief sun was poking itself through the clouds, gradually dispersing themselves, their shadows sliding off the dun colored beach, and skipping off to windward.

I sat for a while on the dock, as it was Saturday morning and I didn't often get the chance to come down to Westhaven.

I could see Pete now making his way down the ramp. I liked Pete. Everyone did. That was the trouble. He walked over toward me slowly and sat down on a piling, as he said, "Hi, teacher, how are all the kids making out these days?"

He sat there passing the time of day. I could see that he was in a talkative mood. There were a lot of interesting things I could ask him about. I asked him about some of the more serious storms, and how long wind kept up at these times.

He told me that a gale blew off Heceta Head uninterruptedly for seven days without abating, with a speed of sixty-five miles an hour. He told also of a eighty mile terror that blew for three days and nights, Nov. 17th, 1937 on Grays Harbor—and said that when the "Alki" was sunk, the storm mashed the housing and entire deck in.

The greatest disaster of all occurred April 8, 1933 when the counted dead was between fifteen and twenty, with seventeen vessels lost.

In a rough westerly swell, the Coast Guard vessel "Troy" saved but one man; the son of the man saved was seen clinging to the front stay. The Coast Guard shot a line to him three times, but each time the boy was too frightened or crazed with fear to let go the stay to grab the line. He was lost before his father's eyes.

At the time of this storm, the hull of the wrecked trawler "Axel" was washed ashore, south of the jetty. Swan Johnson and Axel Backland, both of Astoria, perished when the boat was swamped on the bar. She was hurled on the rocks of the jetty.

Then Pete added, "If you would like to know about the days of full rigged ships, in and around Aberdeen in the early days, you should read *Along The Waterfront* by H. M. Delanty."

I got the book at the first opportunity and felt that I had made the acquaintance of a real Sea Dog, after I had met Red Swanson, and had walked with him down the streets of early Aberdeen. I quote Mr. Delanty:

"A city on pilings with splintery planks underneath, with chandlers having the tar-y, canvassy smell common to all ports of the time.

". . . . There were too the wheels of chance, on which money was won and lost at the return 'of a sail'; there was the tired sailor home from the sea, who looked to the bar rooms and its pseudo glamour, after months of going to sleep with salt crust in his hair. There was swagger that carried playfulness and surcease from the hounding routine of the open sea, to a place of friendship and warmth and companionship, even tho' some were of questionable and dubious nature.

"One welcome was always sure to warm them, when after a quarrel or a disappointment they could forget for the moment in the swishing down of quantities of Wa-hoo water made by the local Indians."

In this early picture patined by Mr. Delanty, the most important of all were the 'bar tugs' that braved the inshore skitter of waves to lead in to Aberdeen ships from 'round the horn.' These ships were sad to hear about, so I said, "Hasn't anything funny ever happened?"

Pete countered with, "Well, there was the time at Clipperton Island when a fierce land crab ate the shoes off the feet of a sailor as he lay sleeping in the sand."

Pete next told me one about a man who is a very popular fisherman here. He said, "You should meet Sid Thorsen who often fishes at Neah Bay, on 'the forties.' He has seen frightening schools of sharks, he told me, 'Man, oh man, was I scared! I just took one look and shut the pilot house door! Man, I never saw such fishing!'"

I looked at Pete and said, "Is that all?"

"Well, there was the skipper who left the ordering of food supplies for two weeks cruise to a green hand. When he arrived to inspect the ship's stores, he found only two cases of pears. He said, 'Hey, Yorge, vere iss de grub?"

"'Dere iss two cases of pars thar.'

"'What, you lug, eat only pears for two weeks?'

"Then the new hand countered with, 'But I like pars!'"

Next Pete told me of the beautiful sea birds found on Bird Island. He told me of the Shags, Gulls and Murs. The Murs, he said, look something like Penguins, the Shags are black and long necked. Next he described the beautiful red headed Sea Parrots, having some orange feathers; these, he said, are found living in the rocks of Bird Island.

We talked for some time now, but I just couldn't miss trying to tease Pete about The Girl! The clouds were gathering again and I thought: it's about time for the rain maker to dust us off. We both got up.

As Pete walked away, he made this remark about girls, and love in general, "Love—love is like hash, you have to have confidence in it to enjoy it!"

I sat there for some time after Pete left, turning this over in my mind! At least this is a great world, and I think Peninsula Pete understood a lot of things. Maybe that is why he was so popular!

I had first dreamed of these lost ships, then I read of them.

Now I was looking out to the darkening sea. I could see the waves breaking over the bar; they looked higher than the shore line. They broke somewhere betwixt the farthest horizon and the sky line. The brisk, rough winds were playing havoc with my hair.

Later, as I sat down on this lonely stretch of beach, I imagined the storm winds breaking over the bar, lifting ships like popping corks and smashing them to their doom. The Westport light held in the palm of her hand the whole parade.

Now I thought of a little girl born on Park Point, Lake Superior, who had looked out and wondered what happened out beyond the light house on the Point. That little girl had been me!

19

The Peninsula, "Lands End"

I motored down th Tokeland at the end of the peninsula, arriving there near sunset. A meager time of day this. A time of gathering together one's forces for the oncoming night. I walked slowly over to the old hotel which it is said had been built about eighty-five years ago.

I thought I would go in and look around. I wondered if the Indian Curio Shop would still be there, as I had understood it had been so long ago. I went and found that the place was being operated now as more of a rooming house. There were no more dinners served regularly now, as there had once been. On the fare side, there was still the dining room with all the tables and clothes, but it now looked desolate and neglected.

There was no cheery room full of people filled with affable camaraderie gracing this room now. There was just the weary wail coming from the baby of one of the tenants.

I looked along the wall where once had been the Curio Shop, the old paintings were still on the walls, but looked out of place, and in keeping with the room as it now was. A few straggly plants much in need of water graced the window sill.

I moved on to the former club house adjoining the hotel—I peeked in the window. The look of the place had a new story, but old to tell.

Merged in front of the stone fireplace was a group of abandoned furniture of little consequence. There were two old trunks with arched brass tops. One of the trunks was partly undone, the straps were not fastened—the lid of the other was thrown back. Some once gay flowered material was sticking out of one side. Even the collar of the dress hung out. I got the impression of a hasty leave-taking, where things not too useful were side-tracked.

I thought of the people who must have made their last meal here. What caused them to leave a disordered trail? Had there been wanton snoopers and ne'er-do-wells who had gone through everything, hoping to find something of value? In front of all was an old rusty cook stove that had perhaps been surrounded by laughing hungry people.

It was hard for me to envision this marked change in the fortunes of this club house. I thought of the happy week-ends that must have been spent here. Of the dances, card playing and jovial toasts that had been given.

Harking back to this past, it seemed to me that this was not real, it was an unwelcome dream, from which I would soon awaken.

Listen!

There is a noise down the stairway, a patter of feet and a hail-fellow-well-met greeting at the doorway. It is eight P.M. and the women are coming in now with the sandwiches, cakes, and pies for the evening.

There is banter from Eric who has been on a long fishing trip. He is ready for a good time.

Tomorrow? There would be plenty of time for sleep then, but tonight, ah, this is tonight. Everything is for tonight. Tomorrow will be another day . . . THE NOISE STOPS . . .

I am back again to the present, the dreary present, somewhere behind the hungry waves breaking over the bar. It is almost dark!

It is today, not years ago, and I stand outside pressing my inquiring nose against the window pane.

There is someone coming up the walk. They are looking for a place to live.

It is said that the OLD CLUB HOUSE is for rent!

20

My Mail

The mail was something that always broke the monotony. There were mail days and mail days.

There was one particular day that I was making a belated return home. It was close to six P.M. I was tired. I had given two music lessons after school.

After I got in the grocery store, I couldn't make up my mind what to have. I looked over the vegetable bins. Some beets caught my eye. That was it—I'd have some beets. To this I added a few other items.

Grabbing the bag haphazardly, I went over to the mail window and asked for my mail. This time there was just a few advertisements and one letter. The writing looked familiar; I recognized it, but not the name that was in the upper corner.

I walked out of the store and down the road slowly, looking toward the harbor and the dying sun. I was so curious about the letter that I couldn't wait to get home to open it. I set the bag of beets down in the middle of the road.

There was a card, on the front of it was a bunch of pansies. The title said, 'Pansies For Remembrance.' I looked inside and saw that it was from Ruth—my long lost Ruth.

We hadn't seen each other in many years. She said that she had seen my name in a Portland paper and wondered if I would remember her!

Where had she been these many years? My mind then took a rapid spin backwards. It all began to come back so vividly.

We had been going with two boys who were in the navy. What a gala time we had.

My parents were often away traveling so we had had things very much to ourselves. We cooked huge course dinners with all the trimmings. We liked to experiment with new dishes, so we had tried them all out on these boys.

They appreciated it, and thought we were splendid cooks.

When the boys were away we flopped dejectedly over our respective mail boxes, with 'that far away look in our eyes.'

The letters were read, and re-read and gloried in.

When there were no boys, as well as no letters, we mooned around listening to soft music. We listened to Jasha Heifitz playing Lange's "Flower Song," "In The Evening By The Moonlight," "Dear Louise" and Victor Herbert's "Kiss Me Again."

The latter proved a real boomerang when one of my brothers grasped the swing door going into the kitchen, kissing it ecstatically, saying, 'KISS ME—KISS ME—AGAH-H-H-en-n-n!"

It was almost more than we could bear, but we thought we could stand anything for our beloveds. We were sunk in an orgy of our own making.

Nothing could bring us out of it. Nothing!

Our mothers reached their wits' end, to know how to cope with this strange malady from which neither of us seemed to awaken. That is except if a new letter came or there would be a phone call from one of them saying they were coming out.

In their absence the weeks flew by, and time was an empty thing.

The only way when there were no messages that we could be brought out of it, was to have some NEW male appear on the horizon.

We now perked up for an evening or two, then lapsed sadly back; especially after comparing notes and finding that 'our beloveds' were so far superior to the new products.

My brothers would say in disgust, "Let's beat it! Here comes the SWEET SUMMER BREEZES!"

We sailed on in our magic land of LOVE, LOVE, LOVE. Here not even the pestiferous small fry could break our enchantment.

So it was Ruth, my dear Ruth. I was remembering now in a mist of tears. I had never forgotten the days we had spent together!

'Could we see each other? Had I forgotten her?'

Just then I heard a car approaching and grabbed my sack of beets to save them from the humiliation of a hit-and-runner.

This freshly turned memory was with me for several days. I found illusive tears making their way down my cheeks at most inopportune moments!

* * *

One week-end when Ruth's father was away on a business trip, I was invited over for dinner.

After dinner we did stunts. Mine was a dance act (for ladies only).

We pushed the dining room table over against the wall. One side of the room was all windows and in addition we put on all the lights. The dining room was secluded, however, by the trees surrounding the house.

I didn't really know what I was going to do when I started out, but as I danced, I thought I'd make it a devil-may-care operation.

My clothes seemed to come off piece by piece, they fell fluttering one by one to the floor as I pranced around looking down coyly at them.

Then I grabbed them up a piece at a time, pulling them, train effect, back of me.

Naturally Ruthie was 'in stitches'—all except me!

21

Metaline Return

There was some difficulty over getting an accommodation at the Davenport in Spokane. The desk clerk told me, if you don't mind taking the large one, there is just one room left.

I, not having the slightest inkling of what was in store, acquiesced. It was a room that had been used for military personnel.

When I was ushered in I noticed that there were three beds. I was so glad to be here that I said nothing as I put on my best smile and handed out a generous tip.

There was a border of circus animals all around the room, a small bar at one end and an apartment size piano at the other. If 'Goldilocks' had been there she could have helped out; I had some difficulty in making up my mind which bed I would sleep in!

I sat down idly at the piano and ran over a few tunes; one especially that I thought appropriate, 'Just picture a Penthouse way up in the sky, with hinges on windows for stars to go by.'

It seemed rather lonely in this big room, and I played this one just to keep myself company. By the time I had run over a few more numbers I wasn't lonely any more!

As I was about to go to bed, I noticed a pedestal lamp. I thought, I'll just put it on to see how it goes.

I turned it on and by some hit or miss, I couldn't get it turned off. It made a large buzzing noise.

I got into bed to see if I could stand it, that is if I had to listen to its heavy rhythm all night. It was no go. I got up again.

After fussing and guming around for about a half hour, I finally succeeded in pressing the proper lever and the darn thing stopped.

Arising early, I caught the buss for Metaline, Washington. I had always loved this place and it seemed like a dream that I was going back to visit after all these years.

The bus wound slowly along the river as we came into higher and higher timber, stopping at each little town along the way. Remembrance came flooding back of all the good times I had had at many of these little places, Blueslide, Jared, Ione, and others. We approached Metaline on the fine new highway that had replaced the old bumpy sliding road.

On arrival I was welcomed with open arms. The years dropped away and it seemed only yesterday that I was holding forth in the little white schoolhouse there.

I came into the small friendly living room where I had enjoyed being an intimate part of this family group. I noticed a certain place on the wall where 'Bergie' had pinned Michael NcNeil's letter to the wall paper, telling me that there was NO MAIL TODAY! I recalled the time she had given me a pretty turquoise ring. I had admired it, laying it carefully on the kitchen table as we were cracking nuts for a cake. We laughed and joked as we worked. We finished and put the nut shells in the stove.

Later, we had looked for the ring but were unable to find it.

The following morning, in cleaning out the ashes, Bergie found the sad remnant of melted gold, and the cracked and smoked stone. We laughed over it but were near to tears at the same time.

This was a token of our friendship; it was indestructible, fire could not burn it away!

That night I went up to the self same room I had occupied so many years ago. I fell asleep to the cheerful sould of the Pend Orielle, spinning itself mysteriously by the back door of the house.

I thought if rivers had memories, the Pend Orielle would remember an impetuous girl daring the mid-stream as it rolled itself down over Dead Man's Eddy.

In retrospect I was swimming the river again with the worried populace on the bank wringing their collective hands in despair over 'that teacher.'

I recalled moonlight nights I had made my way with my escort over the crusted snow in the dead of winter, returning from the town dances.

Yes, it was good to be back to this friendly home of the Burgans and all its fond associations. I had lost both my parents and it seemed that now this was my safe harbor.

There would always be Bergie and Fred; they were home to me now. Fred with his gay French-Canadian ways, his gay laugh. Yes, Fred would always be the same, he would never change, nor would my 'Bergie.' Referring to Bergie, Fred would say, "I marry because HE a good cook!" At the same time winking the corners of his eyes. Then Bergie and Fred and I would all laugh together.

Fred offering to row me across the river to see my friend Dolly Perkins who lived on the other side. Dolly, who you could watch from 'our' side of the river bringing the cows home, going to the barn, but not being able to call loud enough to be heard. Dolly who lived so near and yet SO FAR!

Worried Bergie telling Fred that he must not go. Fred never knowing the loss of his own strength. Fred, why he was strong as an ox. But oh, the river and the eddy below!

Everything was the same. Bergie called me in the morning. On first awakening I thought I must hurry, I will be late for school!

Then I remembered—why this is only a visit!

The real difference was calling Bergie upstairs to zip up my girdle. A side fastener, to give a more svelte look.

A world to slip back into. A world of my youth. An ever widening world. A world that brought joy!

No road could ever be lonely that could have Bergie and Fred at the end. It was not a 'Paradise Lost' but one regained!

22
Alaska

At last I was going to teach in Alaska. I was on the "S.S. Denali," which then made some of the ports in the northwestern part, including the Aleutians.

I arrived at the port of Seward, about 9:30 P.M., Tuesday, September 2. I met many people from other areas in the states; among them were several teachers, enroute to the Aleutians.

I discovered that there would be no bus for Homer, from where I would fly across the bay to Seldovia until the following day, so I would have to wait over, with all my luggage and the two cat cages.

The next morning I was told that there happened to be a mail boat, the "Expansion," leaving for ports 'to westward (the Aleutians); and it would be making a stop at Seldovia. I finally got all my things transferred to the smaller boat, and we waited for about four hours, watching them load the freight and mail. Last aboard were my two cats in their cages, which were lashed to the smoke stack.

I had an inkling when the mate did that, we were going to have none too smooth a passage, but thought no more about it at the time.

There seemed to be nowhere much to sit as this boat was no luxury liner, but we found some benches in the galley. Later we transferred to the bridge-cabin as we watched our craft move slowly out of the Harding Gateway and into the treacherous waters of the Gulf of Alaska.

We rode thus for several hours, until we had supper prepared by two very young Filipino boys. The "Expansion" expected to pick up their regular cook on their arrival at Kodiak.

It wasn't long after dinner that I decided to go below to my bunk, as I had begun to feel more than squeamish. I had never been sick before even on a larger ship. Most of the teachers aboard were enroute to the Aleutians. I shall always be grateful to one of them who helped me in the extremity of my first 'mal de mere' on the beautiful sea that I could not even see! Now it was very dark. She took me by the arm and led me out on deck. I hung on to the scupper stanchions to keep upright, just as the washings of a huge wave came down on my back, as the boat rolled in the trough of the sea. I was wet to the skin, but for obvious reasons, we threw all my clothes overboard, although we managed to save my dress.

I stood shivering in the blackness of the night in the 'altogether' until a blanket was put around me, and I was able to make my way to the ladies room, where for the space of several hours, and sitting on the toilet, I had fallen asleep with my forehead on the wash bowl. As soon as we had left the Gulf of Alaska and entered calmer seas I was able to re-clothe myself and lie on my bunk.

It seemed that I had just fallen asleep when there was a grinding, rending CRASH! I thought of the possible eruption of Mt. Katmai or the coming of the Russians, as I called out "Pray, girls, pray!" The boat had been caught in the tide rip and carried off her course and into an unknown inlet and was scraping on the rocks in the dense fog which had surrounded us on all sides.

Now I put on my coat and went above to see what was cooking— all hands were going about with flash beams to get the lay of the land; the powerful sailing lights had to be turned off as they were too powerful for very close range. The Captain finally placed our position, which was miles off, and after considerable maneuvering, the crew got the ship put to sea again, and full speed ahead.

The first port of call was Seldovia. We hove to, just as dawn was breaking over Seldovia Bay.

My luggage was unloaded and all had to be left at the freight office on the dock until eight A.M. The dock man escorted me to the Hotel Beachcomber, where I was able to get a room pending the finding of permanent quarters; and he returned later with my luggage and the two cat cages—we had taken ash trays from the dock office to feed them.

Later the same day, I was shown the house where I would stay.

It was all done in Sitka spruce and was very modern, with living room, kitchen and bath downstairs. The upstairs had a bedroom alcove with a built in 'bunk bed' equipped with coil springs and mattress. The room was like a small studio; it also had a table that could be used for typing.

The dormer windows looked out over Seldovia Bay, which is

separated from Katchimak Bay by a bight of land surrounded by a small island formations bearing sprice trees.

As I sat typing away I could look out over the harbor, seeing dimly in the distance three beautiful snow covered mountains that are really active volcanoes of the Aleutians, one of which was Mt. Illiamna. The sunsets here are in tints of rose, purple and orange which fires the bay with its reflections, and has no equal anywhere in the world.

The house was surrounded by greenery. The most outstanding was the elderberry which sometimes grows to a height of six feet. The beautiful red berries looked like flowers against the green. There was a riot of raspberries, too, ready for picking.

We got our mail which was flown in to Homer three times a week, later picked up from Homer and brought to us by a small plane crossing the Bay.

The school was situated at the top of a steep hill overlooking the Bay, just above the Standard Oil tanks that held the fuel oil for the stoves of the town and for the fishing craft.

At the time of my arrival the other canneries had shut down for the winter, but the crab cannery was going full tilt. I went down after school one night and got some crab legs, as even the cats and I could not get away with a whole king crab.

My children were of good average intelligence and were a mixture of Indian, Aleut, Scandinavian, and Russian. I had only one child with a Russian name: Kashevaroff.

A small boy greeted me one morning by saying, "My brother sure likes you for his teacher." So there was a tribute worth all the miles I had traveled and even the sea sickness!

The bread at Seldovia had a homemade taste and was the best bread I had ever eaten. There was a bakery in town, and apparel store, movie and two restaurants. Our hotels were The Beachcomer and Seldovia House.

There was a long board walk that extended partly around the harbor area of the town. We had a candy store. The sign read: 'Dodie's Sweet Shop,' and underneath was a note reading: "Gone away for a long weekend." Tsk! Tsk!

At sunset last Sunday, a carillon 'Mass' chimes from the Gospel Mission sounded over the bay; the waters carrying the sound. This greatly moved me, making a picture with gulls wheeling against the backdrop of the sun's downing.

Yesterday at four p.m. a large ocean freighter docked here, the "Square Sinnet," for the unloading of supplies. I took a small girl by the hand and we went down to watch. It was a stirring sight for the child to see, as the crew threw out the hausers and made them fast to the dock, attendant to the mission at hand.

I got up in the night and looked to see if the ship was still there; I saw the shimmer of the lights in the darkness. She waited for full tide the next day at noon and was off, the stern slowly disappearing past the last promontory on the way to the open sea.

There were many incidents that happened that give a picture of my life at Seldovia.

It was late January and I had run out of oil for my range; the man at Standard usually delivered of a Saturday. This Saturday they were very busy at the docks taking on oil brought in by steamer for the hugh oil tank on the hill.

I got some of the older boys later to get the oil for me, which was brought up in a fifty gallon drum. They couldn't get traction with the hand propelled cart on account of the ice, so they rolled the drum up the hill, at angles. The boys were small and only about twelve years old, so we all got into the act, even me. We pushed and rolled, pausing to rest and get our breath. The kids were delighted as they would earn a little 'do-re-mi.' They got a 'lift' out of teacher being along, because—well, wasn't she lots of fun out of school? Really she was just regular people, just like my Mom!" So we were all happy together.

They knew how to open the drum and attach to the connecting pipe on the back porch. Later we all had hot cocoa around! There was 'a rainbow round our shoulders' as we looked down the Bay.

There came another day, and another time. It was early spring, a late afternoon; I hadn't been home from school too long. I was a bit bushed when someone knocked on the back door; I opened the door and there stood the brother of one of my boys. He had his fingers looped through the gills of a ten pound salmon. I was delighted and gave him the two dollars he asked. We were both happy. The beauty of it was, it had been gutted already. The happy smile of this boy was something to behold.

Then, too, there was the time an annivesayr party was given for a Russian couple celebrating twenty-five years. All turned out at the city hall for the dance and festivities attendant to this. Prayers were not offered in the Russian Church as it was only opened this year about twice. This celebration lasted until very late into the small hours, everyone in town assisted and many took part. There was only one piano player in town besides myself, so we took turns. I felt honored to be asked to assist in this.

This special incident I long remembered. I thought to myself, how few teachers have had these unusual experiences. It has often come to mind that a teacher who has had only one school for many years has truly missed out on the finer things of life, these are not bought with money, but in sharing intimately with these children and their families, as here on the far north coast of Alaska.

I, too, have had teaching in the regimented large schools as well as State Correctional and the private schools. There is a special corner of my heart that holds and cherishes experiences in small areas that are most unique! I had great happiness with these charming third and fourth graders; they were cooperative to the nth degree.

We had a small box-like affair on a corner shelf near a window where we fed two pet mice. This morning was extremely cold. We had looked for mama mouse but she was not there. I knew the children were just getting warm so I told them that if they sat quietly I had something to tell them.

I told them mama mouse really talked to me. She said, "Father and I had a terrible time this morning. Our stove pipe fell down and we had a time getting it up again. When we got the fire started, we were both covered with soot, and we didn't want to come up here all messy, that's why we were late showing up." Then she added, "Those cats—well, they don't think we are clean, but we are!"

My feet were so cold I could hardly get up the steps, so we helped each other. You know these basement steps take a lot of climbing."

At this point the children roared, they loved this little tale. I told them many stories from time to time during 'Free Period' Life is really great for children at this age, before they have had to deal with the inconsistencies of later life.

We had our P.E. in the assembly room, where I taught baton twirling, folk dancing, and we put together small plays and skits.

Now we were getting ready for our Xmas program. The mothers always made the costumes for a variety of programs we put on from time to time. This year the general theme was "Frosty, the Snow Man." For this I made black stove pipe hats. We had all the appropriate music for this and also the wonderful carols.

One morning I was working with my ABC's, that is, I was writing the border line around a freshly cleaned blackboard. There are teachers who use cards for this purpose but I guess I was blessed with a very good script of my own. I was busily intent on this and had just reached capitals 'Y and Z'; there was an additional space at the end, my arms were tired, so I just wrote Amen! At that moment, the principal stood in the doorway with his hands grasping the door casing; he was always ready with a quip so he said, "Why Amen?" I was off guard and slightly miffed, so I answered, "Ah, these men?" We both laughed together, taking it in stride, and thought 'Well, just another day.'

We had a bang-up time one New Year's Eve; 'the teachers, the baker, the census taker, and the moccasin man.'

The town had been snowed in the night before. There was about six feet of snow on the rising slopes above the Bay. But Seldovia was in no mood to lose out on their celebration of the New Year.

An old army Jeep left over from the war time helped some of us get 'down town.'

It really wasn't a block and tackle, but a very heavy rope was put around my waist, and I was swung down to the lower level where our Jeep waited. I was very embarrassed but they all teased me, cracking a few jokes as 'Clancy lowered the boom,' which of course had me in stitches. As I got into the Jeep, they added, "Gosh, we thought the rope might break!"

We were greeted with cheers and a glass at each business establishment along the boardwalk; one of which was a sandwich/coctail bar, owned by a prominent citizen of Seldovia.

As we came in we removed our snow boots at the door, and friendly greetings were exchanged. Toward the back there was a small dance floor, on another side were windows looking out on Seldovia Bay.

Some guests had already arrived and festivities were well underway; a square dance was in progress. We joined with them, doing all the old-time dances. Now as we were really warmed up, we gave an eye to the polished floor, and decided to take our shoes off, so several of us danced in our stocking feet.

As the hour of the New Year approached, we formed a circle, hands on shoulders, circling first right, then left. This we repeated several times as new arrivals joined the party. Now we had three minutes to the hour, we urged those who had not taken part, to join. They got into the act, laughing and cheering. As the bells tolled we moved to the center of our circle, cheering and singing: "Should auld acquaintance be forgot and never brought to mind." A tribute here to the people of Seldovia, who were jovial, outgoing and sharing; this was a marvelous and intriguing comradeship!

We departed at three A.M., walking sliding and "Jeeping" homeward bound from this memorable New Year.

*   *   *

There is a dull orange glow settling over the Bay. The air is still and very cold. It is the week after Xmas. The town is seemingly asleep in its blanket of snow. We look up from the board-walk to the buildings on the hill. Far up and very near the top, we see a Quonset hut left there after the war.

Now we see three figures, two men and a woman; we can hear them laughing and talking. The woman is that teacher! She isn't doing too well making the climb, as she has no corks on her boots.

We pause and listen: "Now, Marion, put your flaps down, you are about ready for a landing!"

Just then one of the men loses his balance and makes two slippery bumps as he sprawls on the ridge. This sends a huge cake of snow and ice skittering down the hill.

Now we see a swirl of smoke spiraling up off the hut, into the wild blue—they reach their objective, and later we hear someone playing the piano.

It is the Christmas vacation; some raillery and a heigh-de-hoh! We can hear them all singing, dimly but mistily "I was waltzing with my darlin' to the Tennessee Waltz, when an old friend I happened to see . . . ."

They have forgotten all about the ice, cold and snow. The four of them are having great companionship in spinning their world. They, too, look out toward the Bay and see the distant small island that makes a picturesque setting for this spot they love so well.

23

The Canal and Europe

I was spinning a bit of 'Our World, Yours and Mine' during my summer vacation of 1959. I was aboard the French Line freighter "The Winnepeg" going from Seattle, Washington to Le Havre, France.

Now we were making the final approach to the Canal Zone on June 29, 1959—we arrived before nightfall.

The following morning we awoke to see all the ships anchored in the roadstead to the Canal entrance. There were ships of several nations. We found that there were five ships to pass through the Canal before us. This caused us a delay of about four hours.

In our turn we passed through the Miraflores Locks. It was exciting to see the locks opening on our entry, and the final exit. Lines were tossed with strong cables attached to workers on the Canal side. The ropes were pulled up carrying the cables; the cables were hoisted and hooked on to electric tramway cars carrying at the top large bobbins to which the cable ropes were attached; there were four of these, two amidships and stern and bow lines. The tramcars ran along on tracks, as the ship progressed toward the gates, the bobbins controlling and reeling out the lines.

There were many attendant natives, but I noticed the men on the tramcars appeared to be all white.

There were strips of green lawns between the cement runs. A man was mowing the grass, which must grow overnight in this tropical area.

Now we were in Gatun Lake, moving slowly along. I got a whole roll of color shots of the activity in progress—a fine new freighter of the Johnson Line came into the smaller lock at Miraflores, and tailed us as we passed through Gatun Lake.

Now came Pedro Miguel Lock. After negotiating this, our dinner was served on the top deck, buffet style, so that we would not miss the lovely scenery. As we passed through the famed Culebra Cut, we noticed a large construction company was busy with bulldozers, widening this area, blasting out solid rock in places.

It seemed stirring to have the privilege of witnessing this, after reading about it for so long; one could not help but recall in history the many men who died here to create this lasting monument to the ingenuity of man, that cuts off the miles of ocean lanes around South America!

As we progressed, we noted the jungle growth along the banks, and that the Canal is narrower in some places than some rivers of the world. It was cause for wonderment that it was deep enough to float the very largest vessels; looking back sternward to see as in a fairy phantasia the streamlined red ship of the Johnson Line following at slow pace. The two passed our ship before we reached the last lock.

We heard the twittering of many birds, but did not see them as they were probably hiding under leaves from the tropical sun. I caught a fast glimpse of a little brown monkey playing near the edge of the verdant bush.

By the time we reached the last lock, night had fallen and our five preceding ships were awaiting the go signal. We had been on our feet seven hours, taking pictures and rushing from one side of the ship to the other! We did not miss ANY of the activity. It had been a wonderful, engaging and rewarding day!

Our next objective was to be Willemstadt on the island of Curacao, which we were to reach in two days sailing. Now at five P.M., July 2, we were making the habor approach.

We all craned our necks to catch the first look at Willemstadt, as the ship slowly moved into the Schottegat Basin (deep enough for the very largest ocean vessels). A drawbridge opened to let us through, closed behind us to free cross town traffic going from one side of this quaint Dutch City. Now we were easing up to the dock where we would be about eleven hours taking on fuel oil for the trip across the Atlantic.

We waited paitently for 'Our' shore leave. We would be unable to go ashore until the arriving and checking of customs.

As we were seated, waiting in the library, our French officers 'The Commandant,' Capitane, and chief engineer came in dressed immaculately in tropic whites; they were followed by a coffee-colored man wearing pince-nez, carrying a briefcase.

We watched avidly the procedure of the signing of the port papers. During this interval, two more colored men in uniform came in; one was quite distinguished looking with iron grey hair. They, too, were seated and gave their attention to the business at hand.

Formal greetings were exchanged. Last to enter was a stocky, very blonde Dutchman. Next came the gathering of mail to go ashore; as it was after postal hours, the Dutchman handled the mail, weighing each letter expertly *on his hand* and stating the postage of each. After a short interval, the Commandant had drinks brought in for the port officials. This was our cue to leave.

Looking over the side of the ship, we saw the native dock workers on oil detail, and three very thin dogs. At the side there was a taxi waiting. Four of the passengers got off with me, the driver giving us a volley of *papiamento* (pidgin dialect) giving us a sales talk; in effect saying he would take us on a tour of Willemstadt for eight *guilders;* four dollars American.

The drive over the main streets, through the shopping area, along the Schottegat Basin, and thence up to Fort Nassau at the crest of the hill, will be long remembered.

On our arrival at Fort Nassau area, the driver escorted us up a steep stairway. At one side looking up at the night sky, we could see a row of lighted lanterns, and hear soft enchanting music. We were taken through a narrow areaway where the main restaurant was with adjoining private dining rooms.

We were shown the Peter Styvesant room with the table set for twenty-five in delft china and old Dutch silver. There was a fireplace with a brass kettle swung on tripod giving a historical setting to the room.

As we followed along, we were shown a small airless dungeon, where still could be seen the shackles and ball and chain used on prisoners in the heyday of political occupation and intrigue of the nations that had been involved in the history of Fort Nassau.

As we descended the steps, two soldiers came out and took down the Dutch flag—the sun had just gone down.

We looked down now on the winking lights of small, flat-topped native houses, and larger, more pretentious homes with the lights shining on the flickering harbor waters. This was a vigilant awakening to reality for me.

Now we were driven down the winding streets to see the quiet early evening of this quaint tropical island. The native families in the restful period after sundown. Everywhere we looked we saw the life 'en famille' that appeared (as an Act II on the stage backdrop of a distant time), that was being re-lived for us on this far Caribbean Island, owned by The Netherlands.

Later in the evening, we entered the lobby of one of Willemstadt's finest hotels, a miniature Monte Carlo, complete with baccarat tables, tuxedos and studied faces. There was a small cocktail bar at one side, also a gift shop.

We sauntered through the lobby, then up a circular stairway to the area, where we were told we would find the swimming pool. As we were approaching the top level, we noted round windows which looked into the bottom of the pool; as we reached the very top of the stairway, we could see the pool in complete detail.

It was completely circular and winked like a large green eye at us. We could see the movement of the water in the pool, noting as we walked around it little rivulets of water running over the lights in the floor.

Later we returned to the ship, coming single file up the narrow swinging gangway. We retired at midnight. Tomorrow would be July 4th, and at five A.M. the Chief Steward would check the rooms to see if all were aboard for departure of the ship.

July the Fourth

We were saluted in the morning by small silk American flags on each breakfast table. This gave a heartfelt feeling of home, and was a joyful gesture and salute on the part of our French hosts.

Later at about eleven o'clock, I came down to the library adjoining the dining room—there was quite a rough sea. I was watching from front port windows the heaving and lunging of the ship's bow as it broke water.

My thoughts were of home and the far distance I was to travel. I did not turn around as others entered the room. Then I heard the deck boys turn on a record. First came a dashing melody, just right for the heaving and rolling of the ship, then I heard John Phillip Sousa's "Stars and Stripes Forever." The mid-day gong had rung and as I turned, all stood up and began to sing. A huge American flag had been hung at one side of the archway between the rooms, with the French Tricolor on the other. Tears came to me then, so I turned again to the windows. With the music ringing in my ears and the singing voices, in my mind's eye I saw over the crest of the sea, our American boys marching in close ranks, in the full glory of their youth—smiling faces turned to the colors; but behind each stood the valiant ghosts of 'the real heroes that did not return!'

Coming back to the present, I thought what a wonderful thing it was to recall what our country means to us, in all of its expressions, both joyful and sad!

I WAS A WOMAN WITH A COUNTRY!

24
Rendezvous In Scotland

The most wonderful things happened in Scotland! I arrived on Barra, an island in the Outer Hebrides, July 29th.

The flight from Le Bourget field in Paris was a different experience for me; much conviviality and a glass or two enroute over the English Channel.

On my arrival in Glasgow, coming in from the airport, we were ferried across the River Clyde. A Scottish couple accompanied me and lots of humor passed between us. "Oh, you won't like it on Barra, why you even have to land on a sandy beach, very primitive!" But the husband had a merry twinkle in his eye as he remarked, "Ah now, those McNeils are a bad lot, a very bad lot! You should hear of their adventures during the war!"

The next morning I took the small plane to Barra. We went down first on Tiree, one of the Hebrides; it rolled out like a perfectly flat green carpet dotted with yellow flowers; not a tree visible. This was a stop for re-fueling.

I was looking avidly at the passengers who had descended with me, trying to figure out which ones would be going to Barra.

After we were aloft again, I talked with a man seated aft. He said, "So you are going to Barra? You will have a trip to remember!" He was then, the Clan McNeil trumpeter Allan McNeil-Smith.

As we neared Barra, Allan said to me, "Look down now; presently we will fly directly over the castle and you will see the chief's standard flying from the parapet, as he is now in residence at the castle." Tears came as I looked down, seeing the fairy Castle Kisimul before me, with the standard flying.

I thought of the years my late husband, Michael James McNeil, had been telling me what he had heard from his father about it, and wondering if I would ever see it . . .

We landed then on a perfectly white sand beach, used as the small plane landing strip, a tropical blue North Sea surf breaking before us.

During the course of the afternoon, we were given passes to the Castle bearing our names. The party, reception and ball would be given that evening.

In the dark of early evening, we embarked in Navy P.T. boats (left there from the war) for the Castle, situated on a high lone rock out in the Bay—as we approached the landing area, we were greeted by the Clan Piper, piping a welcome. By flickering lights we gained the Castle entrance, and thence to the great hall.

The scene that greeted us here made one wonder if he were not indeed back in times of early clan history. There were torches in the embrasures of the Castle walls. The exterior of the great hall proper does not show, as we see the Castle on approach from afar.

The curtain wall is about twelve feet thick. Kisimul was begun around the year 1090 A.D. There was a huge fire burning in the fireplace, and on the mantel were great candelabra with gladioli flown in from Glasgow.

An address of greeting was extended from the Chief, Robert Lister McNeil, and he partook of a 'token meal,' thin wafers and wine drunk from a golden goblet of great antiquity; this had been found in the ruins of the Castle during the restoration!

Following this all took part in a varied program of entertainment which included Scottish dances, Gaelic Chants of old, and piping. The solos and piping were presented from the pipers' gallery at the back of the great hall. The chants were continued as those who knew the old songs participated.

Later was the Castle ball when the "Eightsome Reel" and others were presented, bearing resemblance to some of the American Folk dances.

The banquet proper was last; the scene indescribable; the burning torches casting an eerie glow, merging with the time worn light from the glowing logs in the fireplace.

A wall hanging taking up a large portion of the side wall showed in complete detail all parts and colors of the McNeil coat of arms.

At two A.M. we were escorted to the boats to return to Bara. The tide lapping at the Castle walls cast a phosphorescent light as the surf broke on the rocks—The Rock on which Kisimul stands, Alone.

We were several days on Barra. The time was spent in hiking over the rocky boundaries; gaining from aloft the highest point a magnificent and simultaneous view of the North Sea breaking on both beaches, East and West, and the Misty Isles shrouded in their gauze-like covering in the far perspective.

Returning to the hotel, we sat in Congenial close companionship until daylight. A young girl, Valerie Vorzargo, just graduated from the London Conservatory of Music entertained, spontaneously singing arias from several famous operas as she acted the parts, moving gracefully about the room. This was an intensely moving experience for me!

The last night of the gathering, the travelers; McNeils from U.S.A., Australia, New Zealand, Canada and England gave a return party for the Chief and Lady McNeil on Barra. After all had assembled, the entrance of the honor guests was heralded by the Clan Piper.

Now a very informal program was given in which many played a part—even me! I gave them a little Americana, giving my impression of Sophie Tucker singing: "Some of These Days." The Chief remarking "Marion McNeil of Seattle must have been taught that by her mother as I am sure she isn't old enough to have known Miss Tucker!" Tsk! Tsk! (Some diplomacy here, yes?)

The party closed when the Chief and Lady McNeil were piped down to the landing. Following them were all the visiting McNeils in procession, escorting them to their embarkation for the Castle. The travelers—many would depart that evening on the steamer for Glasgow. This scene an unforgettable picture, a bright moon shining over Castle Bay, the lighted steamer with its red stack, the Castle itself in the distance!

Many moving good-byes were said as we bid farewell to our 'companions in arms' who were leaving!

I stayed over two more days, and all motored down the island to see me off. There wasn't a dry eye and the pilot said, typically United Kingdom: "Carry on now! With this emotion I myself might not see my way! These emotional Scots!" . . . . I never dreamed!

25

Kaleidoscopic Memories

(a) Aboard "The Winnepeg"

Just before we had passed Mexico sailing towards the Canal, a main event of the week was the Commandant's Birthday Party. He had included us all in his dinner invitation. We collected a fund and bought four bottles of champagne to be served at the 'tall' end of the evening. The aperitif hour before dinner we had a cocktail party in the library, followed by a roast duck dinner with all the trimmings so well understood by French chefs.

After dinner, we all put on a Vaudeville performance (*par les voyagers*). First was a parody on Little Red Riding Hood . . . A song sung by Bud Sterling "Are You Lonesome Tonight?" . . . I did "Chinatown, My Chinatown" in coolie straw hat and happi coat . . . after the show we had champagne and danced. The second in command known as the 'Captain' and I did a dance in the style of the flamenco with a bull fight sequence. (Pause here for breath!) We all signed off at midnight and went on deck for star gazing . . . Overtones here of Martinique Rum . . . My! My!

Leaving the Mexican coast, the Commandant had the swimming pool filled for us. I had done a lot of talking about my ability in the water . . . I even told them I could hold a glass of wine between my ankles, swim on my back across the pool and not spill any! The passengers smirked around a bit, and I could see with their winking looks, they had reservations about this.

The following morning we were all summoned to the aft deck; we saw a notice posted at the stairway up to the pool. It read: *MARION EXCLUSIVE*, pool hour 11:00-11:30. We all hurried to get ready.

After much attendant banter, I dove in, turned on my back, bringing my feet to the surface, and putting my ankles together. One of the men waded in carrying the partly filled glass. He placed it between my ankles. Now all held their respective breaths—me too! I spun off fanning both hands, propelling myself slowly across the pool. Of course I spilled some but hadn't let go of the glass. One of the men reached for it and all gave me a 'hand.' I did all my stunts and some took movies, also pics in color.

At dinner that night, all stood and sang: "We're in love with you, Bubbles, say you love us too, Bubbles," to the tune of "Honey." This was a high point for me and I had difficulty holding back the tears!

If any of my readers who were passengers on "The Winnepeg" see this, they will remember.

(b) An Artist's Letters

18 St. Peter St., London
Sept. 5, 1968

Dear Marion,

I am at East Beach Promenade at Southend-On-Sea. This is a peasants' resort, thirty miles east of 'East London' (the ghettos). No swank hotels, but lovely Georgian hotels with the inevitable terrace.

There is a southwest breeze; all day super cloud formations, thunder over the Isle of Sheppey, twenty miles southeast of the pier.

There are people here who work at 'Briton's Ford Cars' from Dagenham (Thames side) in thousands. I look out toward the pier, and at the end on the right, there are Anglers after mackerel. Now I look out to sea. A ship, the "Lock Paul" is enroute to Vancouver, B.C., Canada.

. . . Now for me into the Royal Oak for English ale, a half pint. After dark the illuminations came on! The whole Promenade was alight for three miles, the Great White Way!

* * *

Again Charles writes:

October 24, 1970
11-Bondway, London, U.K.

Dear Marion:

I am in George's Chapel. Windsor, "My look at that," a U.S. girl says to the others! (Is there nothing in U.S. to compare) . . . As I have been reared on all this, I suppose I am skeptic, so I must keep out of the New World? Yes?

I am going to London Bridge today to see the great demolition. As the old is demolished, the new is replaced. It will be erected again, piece by piece, in Arizona, U.S.A. The old world sheds the old and gives the new world this approbrium! Hi! Here we are, New World! Your chance for the Gold! Tsk! Tsk!

I made five English landscapes. Trees—a stone bridge—a thatched cottage—a U.S. traveler says: I have 'soul': a copy for you, Marion, at the end of the season. I sold a super scene at Piccadilly Circus to a party from Santa Monica, California.

Cheers,
Charles J. Pierce.

(c) On Leaving Europe

Five days in Paris and environs, day trips to Fontainbleu, Malmaisan and Versailles, Fun at Les Halles (French Market) where we had the famous onion soup and white wine.

As we came out now at three A.M., it begins to be daylight. Produce trucks are rolling in, parking at the curbs. Passersby notice our inherent raillery—a gay *"Comment ce vas?"* and jolly waving. I join their line and heft one or two of their sacks of produce myself! Silly me—Our group yelling, "Marion, for heaven's sake, let's go!" M-M-M. The following evening we are standing at the curbside of the Eiffel Tower; it is eight P.M. and suddenly the lights come on! Behold! . . . Now we are on an American Express Bus bound for the Lido, all are singing "Clancy Lowers The Boom." A Sunday afternoon sitting under the Arc de Triumph, reading names of all the illustrious generals who served in the campaigns of Napoleon, as well as the famous Generals of World War Two.

I flew home, non-stop, London to Seattle, Washington in nine hours. Seeing the Sun Rise over the glacial ice of the region north of Canada—a dream, Yes! But home now! The sight of Our Flag!

All I wished for most now was just a hot dog and a piece of apple pie!

26
Epilogue

Many times going home from school in the winter there was a heavy gale blowing. I tied up my head well, buttoning my coat against the force of the wind.

I stopped at the store to get a few necessities for the coming night and morning. The wind was blowing so hard that the matter of breathing was a real 'putch.' I held my breath for a moment, then gulped several deep breaths at a time.

I went in to the service station to make a long distance call to seattle. I was waiting for a return on my call when a boy came in. He had something in a shoe box. I said, "What have you got there?"

"Oh, my kitten."

"Let's see it."

He took the lid off the box, but the cat did not move. I asked, "What's the matter with it?"

"Oh, he's dead, he got run over this morning!"

It was curled up and looked as if it was sleeping.

"When are you going to bury it?"

"Oh, tonight sometime." It was all nestled in the tissue paper.

He looked into the box lovingly and I wondered what his thoughts were. A little boy and his dead kitten!"

When I reached home I put the groceries down, took off my coat, shaking off the water and put my scarf up to dry.

I sat then for a few minutes, looking out the window of my 'castle' toward the harbor.

A giant fir was swaying in the gale. It was fun to watch the storm sweeping the mammoth branches against the sky. The winter dusk was pervaded also by the muted hoot of the fog horn.

I could see the flashes of car headlights as they made their way across the Elk River bridge.

To the lulling dirge of the storm I fell asleep.

When I awoke the room was cold and my neck was stiff. The storm was whipping up to a crescendo. Water was coming in around the windows.

I put my robe on for extra warmth, turned on the radio and put on the electric plate to make my supper.

I did the usual things with cans and made a pot of tea. A glow now settled over the room. I had fixed a warm little dinner and the tea pot was burping steam.

After dinner I got into one of my usual books, forgetting for the moment all about the wind.

The hours slipped away.

The storm was increasing in intensity. As I peered out through the window, I could see the lashing water in the distance under the bridge, the lights of which were wavering blurs on the water.

Now I began to undress for bed.

Taking off my 'Sloppy Joes,' I shook the sand out of my shoes. I pounded the heels on the floor to be sure of doing a good job. Then I ran my fingers the full length of the sole in scraping off the fine particles.

I took off my socks, running my fingers between each toe. There was always sand there every night.

With a heavy tiredness, I thought: sand-sand-sand. There always seemed to be sand in my shoes.

I thought of the nights I had sat there religiously taking the sand out of my shoes.

Why wouldn't that be a good title for my book? Sand In My Shoes, I thought.

I couldn't put the thought away—the shore lines, even as far back as Lake Superior, the shore lines I had traveled and the repeated performance of the sand!

I slipped into bed with the wind beating a merry tattoo on the window. I heard faintly and more faintly the wail of the fog horn.

I was carried away, and in a dream I was drifting off on a huge sand dune, which seemed to sail away like a magic carpet.

*   *   *

The schoolhouse seemed the same to me. I walked in and sat at my desk.

There was a group of my little children waiting with their readers at the back of the room.

I took a book and walked back to them.

They looked up with alert and inquiring glances. Someone asked, "What page?"

I didn't answer, I couldn't—I seemed so far away.

I heard then some little mimblings, a slight disagreement as to the page.

One of the children stood up and began to read in a confident voice.

It was Kenny, with his little rosy face poring intently over his book.

The voices droned on.

I looked out of the window, seeing the tops of the trees undulating in the wind. A storm was blowing up on the peninsula.

It began to rain and the voices of the children softened and I heard a small piping voice.

THE VOICE WAS SINGING: "It isn't raining rain, you know, it's raining violets."

Now the voice died away. I had returned to my babes.

Someone was saying, "What page, teacher, what page?"